RAMBLES

INTO

SACRED

REALMS

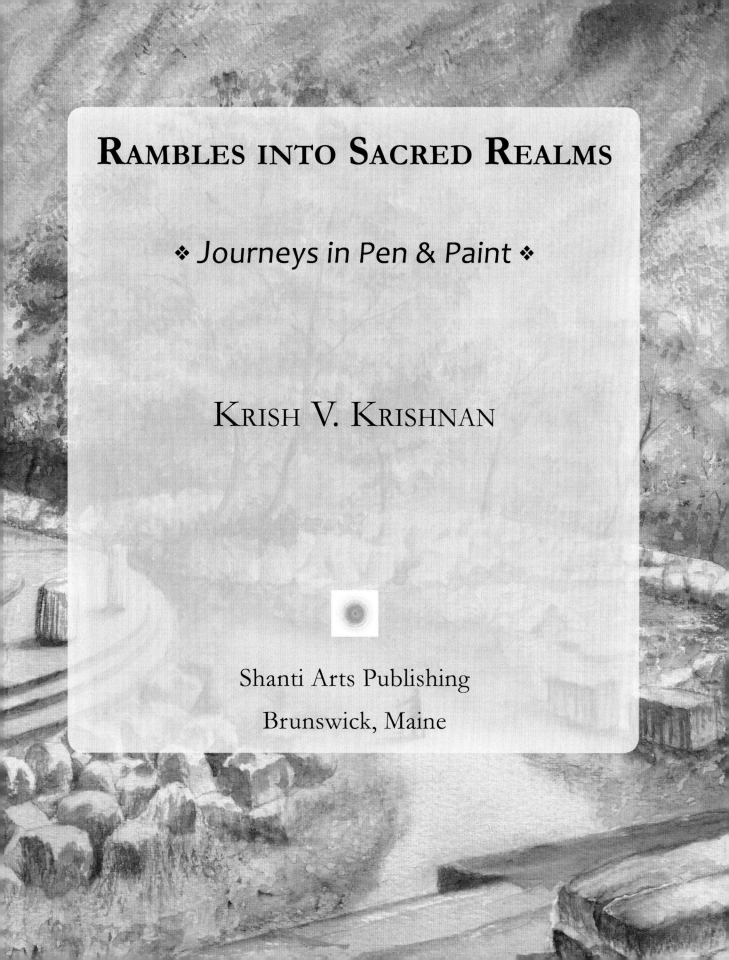

RAMBLES INTO SACRED REALMS

❖ *Journeys in Pen & Paint* ❖

KRISH V. KRISHNAN

Shanti Arts Publishing

Brunswick, Maine

RAMBLES INTO SACRED REALMS: JOURNEYS IN PEN & PAINT

Published by Shanti Arts Publishing
Cover and interior design by Shanti Arts Designs

Shanti Arts LLC
193 Hillside Road
Brunswick, Maine 04011
www.shantiarts.com

Printed in the United States of America

First edition

10 9 8 7 6 5 4 3 2 1

Library of Congress Cataloging Information (forthcoming)

To the divinity that surrounds us.

ACKNOWLEDGMENTS

I have many people to thank for my years of travel experience, inspiration, and hard-earned wisdom. First and foremost, my family genes have enabled me to document my impressions through pen and paint. In particular, I'm grateful to my father, who has kept his art alive despite age and adversity, and my late uncle, who authored his own book over thirty years ago. Both men have been great sources of inspiration.

No words can express my immeasurable gratitude to my dearest friend, guide, and wife, Ramaa, who first suggested the idea for my book and has encouraged me every step along the way, even as we changed cities, countries, and continents over the years. My son, Anish, bore in large part the brunt of my travel eccentricities as we moved him from school to school across Bangalore, Bangkok, Tel Aviv, and Chicago. My daughter Amrita, an artist herself, patiently keeps me company through my painting hours at my studio, offering unvarnished critiques as well as hue suggestions to her partly colorblind father!

I am indebted to my editor Lisa Pliscou for reviewing my chapters several times over and for being a fount of guidance through my hardest journey of all — the trek to get my first book published! I would also like to thank my publisher, Christine Cote, who truly believed in me and my book; my sincere appreciation goes to her and her editorial staff who patiently went through several rounds of editing, lending a high level of grammatical polish to my work.

Lastly I would like to thank those unsung heroes of my travel years: the many guides who so often made the dullest historical fact exciting with their colorful narratives, accompanying me to the most isolated spots on the planet, and patiently waiting it out during my inspirational moments as I lagged behind taking photographs or making sketches in the spur of the moment.

There are many others who have helped behind the scenes, and to try to mention them all would risk turning this page into a full chapter! However, you know who you are, and I thank you most sincerely.

Without any single one of these wonderful people, my book would never have become a reality.

Krish V. Krishnan
Chicago, Illinois

CONTENTS

INTRODUCTION

I could not have been in a holier setting than the one that stretched before me.

I was perched high upon a stone parapet, facing the Western Wall, and isolated from the incessant tromp of tourists. The morning sun glistened upon the Dome of the Rock. Throngs moved below in hushed prayer. Within seconds I heard footsteps behind me. An instinct made me look up. I was surrounded by a posse of gun-toting Israeli soldiers, one of whom seemed very suspicious that I was carefully creating a blueprint of the area — probably for some murky reason.

Remembering a sage piece of advice from a forebear about never looking a feral dog in the eye, I simply continued with my artwork as if nothing unusual was happening. I hoped my shaking hand wouldn't betray me.

Thirty suspenseful minutes later, I packed up my art paraphernalia and casually ambled away, at which point so did the soldiers. With my limited Hebrew lexicon I understood one of them to say something to the effect of: "Did we scare him away?"

An acrylic drawing is my unforgettable reminder of that day, but I never recreated a formal painting from that color sketch, which still hangs in my studio in Chicago.

Once, sitting on stone steps among the tree-strangled shrines of Ta Prohm in Cambodia, I was engrossed in painting when I suddenly heard a rustle, only to catch a glimpse of a glistening cobra slithering right between my shoes. I gasped and jerked to my feet, splattering my palette all over my formerly impeccable beige trousers that had now become an unfortunate canvas for abstract expressionism.

There was the memorable afternoon in the desert when I agreed to what was supposedly a rarely offered camel tour around the Pyramids. An hour later, as I sat perched precariously upon a wobbly hump, my formerly affable Egyptian guide was gesticulating wildly and threatening to walk the camel even further into the Libyan Sahara where, he warned me, I would never be found — unless I paid him a premium.

As I've crisscrossed the globe, both for business and pleasure, places of divine power have always intrigued me, drawn me, and led me into inspiration and adventure. From the mighty red rocks of Petra, to the fury of the Hawaiian volcanoes, and the religious fervor of Varanasi, I've long been compelled to explore and portray these awe-inspiring places of divinity through my writing and artwork.

Places that inspire me typically have an air of spiritual mystery about them. Over the years I've sought out havens of worship around the globe: divine nooks of nature, the mythological theaters of gods and goddesses, the man-made towns and monuments consecrated by devotion, legends, and time. Some of these spots are wrapped in silence; in others, thousands congregate to experience the elation of something beautiful, something elevating.

Through my artwork and writing I seek to portray the emotional essence of such places. It's less about how they might appear to the casual observer than how they feel to me at that moment of thrilling inspiration.

I'm often asked how long it takes me create my artwork. "It all depends," I inevitably reply. Inspiration is so fleeting, yet so powerful. I never know when the onrush will hit me, and I may be ten thousand miles away from the place I suddenly want to recreate. Sometimes it takes me hours to finish a piece, but it could also be days, weeks, or even months, especially when I'm compelled to go there again for yet another encounter. I'm very particular about selecting the media that feel right at any given time, whether it's acrylic, watercolor, pastel, scratchboard, pencil, or ink. Unlike words that can be scrawled on a paper napkin in a pinch, executing artwork takes patience and, sometimes, courage.

In some cultures, a person holding a brush to canvas makes for a curious sight, provoking prying stares or drawing a crowd in a huddle at close quarters. The bolder spectators happily offer to pose for a portrait "at no extra charge." Under these uncomfortable circumstances, I often resort to a hurried sketch or even a click of the camera, only to complete my artwork in the lone comfort of my hotel room or studio.

In some places, there's an element of risk in seeking just the right vantage point. From goliath beetles, spitting cobras, and feral dogs in dense jungles to armed militants in political tinderboxes, there are risks I take, but in the high of the moment, these seem inconsequential compared to the delight of simply being there.

Why don't you simply take photos?" curious acquaintances often ask, eyeing my messy studio strewn with paintbrushes and palettes, pencils scattered on color-blotched rugs poised to prick the unwary, and a riot of handwritten notes flapping in the breeze through an open window.

With today's gadgetry, I could easily capture that matchless moment with a compact smartphone. It does seem odd that I spend hours all alone in far-off lands, often under a blazing sun, companion to inquisitive fauna and an overly friendly insect world, using a brush or scratchboard knife to document something that, at least until recently, relatively few have seen.

However, there is something deeply personal and immensely rewarding in what I do during the hours I spend freezing that exhilaratingly precious moment on canvas and scribbling thoughts in my notebook. With each deliberate brushstroke or scratch of the knife, I'm keenly tuned in to the very moment I am recreating, losing myself in the profound joy of the subject before me. And when that subject is something divinely awe-inspiring — like lava gushing untrammeled out of a volcano deified as a goddess, or the timeless columns of a hallowed Grecian temple against the backdrop of verdant olive groves, or the vibrant throb of devotion in a city of ancient cultures — this act becomes one of spontaneous submission to the sublime.

Decades of incessant travel, painting, and writing have transformed me in ways both large and small. My wanderings have changed how I interact with family and friends, guests from across a border, and acquaintances from distant lands. Close to home, it has changed even the way I think of myself.
I've come to enjoy the adventure inherent in uncertainty and have developed more patience, tolerance, open-mindedness, and adaptability. I've gained a deeper

understanding of human beliefs and learned to look past differences in color and credos, coming to the simple yet profound realization that at the end of the day, despite all our superficial differences, despite the divisiveness that can be created by religion and politics, everyone around the globe is really the same.

Thanks to my rambles, the world has become to me a wonderfully small and familiar place.

In search of something special, I have crossed international borders by plane, bus, train, and boat. While getting there is usually uneventful, very often I have stumbled into unexpected barriers laced with conundrums of culture and language. As you'll read in this book, while some experiences have been humorous, others have been harrowing, often leaving an aftermath of fear and angst.

In the process I've learned quite a bit about people and their practices, and am truly amazed by the many ways we think and speak. While touching someone on the head is a blessing in my native India, such a gesture in sacrilege in nearby Thailand. In many parts of the Middle East, you never touch food or even the table with your left hand, and you never acknowledge a scrumptious lunch with a thumbs-up sign! Several wallets lighter, I've come to understand that haggling techniques vary greatly by the country I'm in and also depend on whether I am on solid ground or helplessly perched upon a camel in the middle of the desert.

Before I began my international peregrinations, I had no idea there were over a hundred funny variants of English spoken around the world, including Manglish (in Malaysia), Yinglish (English and Yiddish, of course—don't be a shnuk!), Singlish (in Singapore), Hinglish (in India), and Thinglish (Thailand's patois that I really enjoyed speaking).

Exposed to the strangest of tongues during my travels, I'm often possessed by a burning desire to speak them. I pack old-school, dog-eared phrasebooks along with my palette, toothbrush, and shaving cream. My stuttered attempts at someone else's language often elicit a controlled giggle or even outright laughter. Printed words won't tell you that Thai is a tonal language sprinkled with grammatical minefields or that Mandarin and Cantonese have a lilt to them, flowing like India ink applied with a delicate brush.

All my life I've been fortunate to have participated in spiritually powerful celebrations that have had a deep impact on me. Growing up in India, I relished the excitement of Diwali day, the Hindu festival of lights. At dawn we would set off fireworks that exploded high above in a dazzling blaze of colors. Thus is darkness banished by light, just as goodness triumphs over evil. Later, living in Thailand with my family, we never missed the November evening, illuminated by a full moon, walking along the crowded banks of the Chao Phraya River as the faithful launched krathongs, boats fashioned out of banana leaves, laden with candles, flowers, and joss-sticks, accompanied by prayers, hopes, and wishes. During the time spent in Israel, our friends and their families celebrated Hanukkah in December with candelabras representing the eight continuous nights that a flame, against all odds, burned in an ancient temple — a holy miracle.

Sometimes, at unexpected moments, I experience soul-stirring events that feel as sacred to me as the man-made celebrations of religions and faiths. In the Alaskan tundra high above the Arctic Circle, I witnessed nature rejoicing in its cherished moments in quiet ceremony. As the sun sinks into torpid slumber, cold winter shrouds the land in what will be months of secret darkness. Suddenly the sky is illuminated by breathtaking bands of green, lilac, blue, and purple—as if some exuberant artist is splashing colors on a celestial canvas, lighting up a desolate world.

These—and more—are the moments of divinity I strive to capture through pen and paint.

Why does divinity matter?

It matters because we live in a world crazed by computers and clocks. We head out to the IMAX Theater or to an office party, driving long distances, biting our nails, and cursing the traffic, but rarely do we pause to really see wildflowers in the meadow, the promise of tulips shying out of the March mud, or a golden sunset in the skies. Instead we tend more to notice a world cleft by manmade schisms of race, beliefs, and religions, fostering the darkest deeds of war and terror.

I have wandered the world enough to know that things need not be this way.

There is divinity in the most mundane moments, the most ordinary places around us; it uplifts us, binds us together, and can waken us to the indescribable beauty of our planet.

One feels a sense of calm elation in watching the moon rise over Lake Michigan on a wintry evening, the very moon that at the same instant is setting below the dunes of the Kalahari desert, being watched by Bedouins on their weary camel caravans. As the sun rises above the lilied ponds of Angkor, it simultaneously illuminates the skies of New Hampshire as it drops below its cloud-capped mountains.

Similarly, many find a quiet sense of fulfillment while listening to a sermon at church or the pealing bells of a lakeside shrine. For thousands of years and in a multitude of ways, we have sought encounters with the divine in temples, cathedrals, mosques, Buddhist viharas, synagogues, and mountaintop monasteries. We have infused holiness into these places through collective worship and prayer.

We also seek out the sublime in Mother Nature's most hallowed shelters — some of which are powerfully sacred for reasons truly unknown. Somewhere amid the lush olive groves of Delphi, where the Oracle once held sway, lies the sacred omphalos, the hallowed navel of the earth. Deep inside the caves of Actun Tunichil Muknal, the Maya fervently called out to their gods through pain-filled rituals. Worshippers were spellbound by the cataclysmic might of the goddess Pele as she bursts out in red rage from her volcanic abode in Hawaii.

These are the shades of divinity I have for many years sought humbly to explore through pen and paint.

Each set in a different country, the twelve chapters of *Rambles into Sacred Realms* are distillations of my artwork, travel writings, and moments of personal insight, all documenting my travels over a period of thirty years. I've lived in these cultures, imbibed their legends and languages, and engaged the services of expert local guides to help me better comprehend and appreciate native perspectives on what makes these places and their experiences so special.

My hope is to take you with me to these enchanting destinations to vicariously enjoy the adventure, the drama, and the humor illuminating my travels, as well as to provide an opportunity to experience — through the perspective of my words and images—the stunning power of these incredible places.

And who knows? Maybe, if you're not already doing so, you'll be inspired to seek your own places of awe and connection — near or far. Perhaps you'll begin to capture your experiences through drawing, painting, writing, photography, poetry, or other forms of meaningful personal expression, just as I have done throughout this book.

Should I or Should I Not?: At the Entrance to the Cave

Scratchboard, 9 x 12

"Hurry! Seats will get filled fast" was the urgent advice offered to me at the hotel where I was staying. This call caused me to scramble to the front desk with my credit card, get my entire family signed up for the daylong adventure, and gather everyone into a waiting minivan. ❖ Little did I realize what this would mean: swimming, scrambling, and climbing. While my son, Anish, then fifteen years old, was probably capable, Amrita, my daughter, just nine, was a shade too little for such physically harrowing adventures! ❖ Until I visited Actun Tunichil Muknal, I had always thought of sacred caves as museums of sorts, where peaceful monks played with pigment and chisel, transforming stones into history. After walking, hiking, and wading through virgin landscape for what seemed like endless hours, we came upon a spectacular cave riddled with vines and foliage. A small monkey seemed to amuse itself, jumping across the branches. But my heart sank at the sight in front of me. Just inside the hourglass-shaped entrance to the cave, I saw a guide with a headlamp egging on a couple of reluctant tourists to travel deeper into its dank depths. As far as I could tell, they seemed to be faint-hearted and fearful. ❖ There was no camera to take a picture with since these were all packed in tough polyethylene wrap that Orlando, my hardy guide, chose to lug. I had to make a mental note, especially of the little capuchin monkey who seemed to be now mocking my upcoming attempt at adventure. ❖ A few months later, I used scratchboard to convey the sense of dark mystery in the cave.

CHAPTER ONE

BELIZE ❖ ACTUN TUNICHIL MUKNAL

SECRETS FROM A SCARY UNDERWORLD

Some cultures have used sacred caves as gateways to a holy netherworld. Hundreds of years ago, severe droughts left the Maya desperate and anxious to appease their frightful gods of the subterranean realms. While muttering incantations, shamans with torches, their victims in tow, entered the deep and dark cave, wading through these same waters and clambering over the same rocks on which I was now struggling.

After a visit of about two hours, I stumbled into a welcome gleam of sunlight and back into this century. I was simply glad to be alive, unlike some of past civilizations who had lost their way or, worse still, became hapless sacrificial victims who had no choice but to be left behind.

The entrance to the hourglass-shaped cavern loomed ominously. There was much to fear since I would soon be venturing into the kingdom of angry gods.

Fully clothed and with tennis shoes on my feet, I jumped awkwardly into the turquoise waters, swimming up to a ledge leading into the cave's dark belly. As the gush of the aptly named Roaring Creek angrily pushed me back against the slippery rocks, a wave of hesitation welled inside. Was I ready to take on the dark secrets of the Maya netherworld?

Mother and Child: A Family Portrait

Scratchboard, 16 x 20

Hiking the densely-forested terrain of the Cockscomb Basin Jaguar Preserve in Belize, I spotted several troops of howler monkeys, gibnuts, white-lipped peccaries, and countless exotic birds. Sadly the only jaguar I spotted on that trip was at the Belize Zoo. ❖ Not as yet content with such an interesting animal parade, my ears perked up at every rustle in the thicket and every faint whistle in the brush. Having once rubbed shoulders with the ancient Maya, the Baird's tapir indeed proved to be a shy creature. A scary herbivore when enraged, I had to be careful lest I stumble upon an unsuspecting full-grown adult or worse, a mother and its baby. ❖ Unfortunately, the closest I came to spotting a mountain cow, as the tapir is known, was only a set of fresh tracks on a trail leading to a pond. ❖ My foray to the Belize Zoo surprisingly proved futile since the resident tapir had decided to spend its afternoon napping. ❖ Determined, I ended up at the Field Museum in Chicago, picking up where the taxidermist had left off. ❖ Using scratchboard to immortalize this unusual creature, I used an X-Acto #11 blade, nicking out each strand of fur, hair by hair. One of the biggest pieces I had ever attempted in this medium, it took me several weeks to complete the mother and child portrait.

I felt I had to try.

Biting my lip, I whispered to our guide that I didn't know how to swim! Dismissing all apprehensions, the dauntless Orlando confidently assured me that my loaner lifejacket was all that was needed to see me through such a harrowing adventure. Clambering upstream among gigantic stones and squeezing through sharp calcite formations, it seemed to me that time was slowing down. Our party of eight was wading through neck-deep waters into the world of an ancient people.

I had just driven from San Ignacio in western Belize to this spot where a large Maya civilization flourished more than fifteen hundred years ago. Upon this tract, a lush forest now teems with the squeals of keel-billed toucans and growls of howler monkeys. For an hour, we plodded through the Tapir Mountain Nature Reserve, where a rustle could hide a shy tapir chewing on the bushes or even a crouching jaguar. We had made three river crossings already, and our guide goaded us on.

Had I foolishly signed up for an adventure suitable only for the hardiest?

We were headed to a timeworn Maya sacrificial site known as Actun Tunichil Muknal — Cave of the Stone Sepulcher. In 1989 a farmer stumbled upon this site. Soon archaeologists came to explore an area deep into the cave, and afterwards, it was opened to the public in 1998. Not long ago, the czars of adventure themselves, National Geographic, offered an expedition into this site, branding it an utter "place of fright."

A Subterranean Adventure

This maw of the Maya underworld was remarkably well preserved. After that first, awkward swim into the cave, the world seemed enveloped in a stifling darkness as all sunlight was shut out. We moved single file, clinging to one rock after another, relaying the next danger ahead to the person behind. I moved cautiously, yet the jagged boulders kept scraping my knees and warned me that the next obstacle could be a rock that would gash my leg open. Yet all danger was hidden by rushing water and darkness.

Incredible secrets were unveiled upon those stone walls as the small group of adventurers splashed through cold waters and clambered over rocks, guided only by

Caves are not lonesome places; they abound, in fact, with a thriving ecosystem. Fruit bats that communicate through echolocation coexist with creepy crawlies like the scorpion or the wolf spider. There are eyeless species, such as the blind cave fish or salamander that have discarded useless sight in favor of other senses. Cave moss, lichens, and glowing fungi provide nutrition to such denizens of the darkness. ❖ Contrary to my innocent images of isolated hermits using caves as canvas, some cultures used these as gateways to a holy world below. As I ventured deep into spectacular Actun Tunichil Muknal, swimming against Roaring Creek, scrambling among jagged rocks, and squeezing through narrow crevices above the roar of the water, I entered an unimaginably vast chamber laden with stalactites, stalagmites, and flowstones. To my eye they were nothing less than iridescent adornments. ❖ This flowstone formation must have been at least fifteen feet tall. As it glittered and glowed in the light of my headlamp, I couldn't help thinking what the Maya victims would have felt as they were whisked past these wonders towards their doom. ❖ I wanted to capture the essence of the natural monument and its powerful visage of bulbous rock. I used a charcoal stick to make a sketch in ten minutes.

Speleological Spectacle: A Massive Flowstone

Charcoal, 12 x 9

the conical spots cast by headlamps. The glow from these lamps caused the limestone to glitter and the flowstone to sparkle, and I noticed the blur of artifacts scattered just as the Maya had left them over twelve centuries ago.

Intense droughts between 700 and 900 C.E. caused a great deal of suffering among the Maya, and they were convinced the gods needed to be placated. Weeklong festivities at the cave's mouth would propitiate these divinities as well as the mystical Ceiba tree spreading

A Rare Guest?: Feisty Harpy Eagle

Watercolor, 14 x 10

As we were crossing Roaring Creek by the Tapir Mountain Nature Reserve, Orlando, our guide, spotted a huge bird gliding in the skies. He swore it was one of the critically endangered harpy eagles, though I wasn't too sure. I did know that these powerful eagles can easily lift and fly off with a sloth or monkey and are one of the most powerful raptors that live in these parts. ❖ My curiosity stirred, I wouldn't let Hugh, my San Ignacio guide, easily off the hook. A couple of days later, I made it a point to stop at the famous Belize Zoo where there was a pair of harpy eagles in captivity. As I neared one of these magnificent birds, he savaged me menacingly, smashing the cage with such force that I backed off instantly. His feathers were glistening against the filtered sunlight. ❖ I was fascinated by his regal bearing and the way he looked at me with a "come and try me" look. ❖ I sketched this later with a pencil on a pad. I used dry brush on cold-pressed watercolor paper to create the texture of the feathers.

its branches to the heavens. Alas, its dark roots led to dreaded Xibalba, the underworld whose gatekeepers weren't easily sated. They needed human blood.

Torches in hands, muttering arcane incantations, the shamans who had been feasting on hallucinogenic mushrooms splashed into these very waters with their hapless victims, effortlessly navigating their way through rushing torrents and razor-sharp stone. Their tall headdresses, laden with feathers of the sacred quetzel bird, must have

Evil Banished

Pastel, 9 x 14

As I stumbled precariously upon slippery rocks, I came upon this collection of ancient artifacts. Orlando explained that droughts would be accompanied by gruesome bloodletting rituals. One such ceremony had kings and queens piercing themselves with stingray barbs in a bid to appease the subterranean gods. In another, people shattered pots against rock in the belief that evil spirits would banish themselves from their lands, letting rain pour and good fortune return to their parched kingdom. ❖ Orlando's narrative was horrific and stirring. A few broken pots still lay on the cold floor, testament to one of those days when desperate Maya would have congregated here conducting their gory rituals. The cave resounded to the clangor of shattering pottery on its stony floor. I spotted an intact "Monkey Pot," one of the few found in these parts, a clay container with a small monkey embossed upon its face. ❖ A pastel drawing seemed to be the best medium to capture the effect of scant light inflicted upon darkness.

A Horrific Death: Victim of a Sacrifice

Scratchboard, 5 x 7

Fourteen skeletons lay sprawled in front of me. Others had likely been washed away in the floods. ❖ *A lone skull had been separated from the rest, and a couple of stray thighbones lay scattered on the floor. A powerful lamp cast an eerie shadow, and the contrast of the glistening skull in that overpowering darkness was astounding.* ❖ *I couldn't get myself to depict this in any medium other than a black and white scratchboard. It conveys so well the stark contrast of powerful light and utter darkness.*

slowed them down. As I made my way along, it almost seemed I could hear the fervent chants of that ominous entourage amidst the cacophony of the gushing waters.

Several large jars laden with offerings were likely lowered down the sky-lit opening we encountered a quarter mile into the cave where the roof had collapsed. Here I saw a horrific assortment of bowls and instruments for bloody rituals I didn't care to think about.

Squeezing through narrow crevices, we entered a stunningly vast chamber. We were asked to walk barefoot, for this was the sacred sanctum of the ancient Maya. In all my years of travel, this ghastly cathedral of nature was one of the most remarkable sights I have ever seen (right).

Here was a huge stone hall with stalactites, stalagmites, and flowstones as coruscating adornments. Scattered on the floor were skulls and bones, just as the ancients had left them after their horrific deeds. Only swaths of protective masking tape separated our century from theirs.

The skeletons of fourteen sacrificial victims lay sprawled here (page 25). There were probably many more that had been washed away in floods or buried atop a ledge somewhere. Some were children and infants from noble families, known because of their cranial modifications. Our guide told us that the elite Maya clamped wooden plates clamped on a baby's forehead to create flatness above the eyes, which was considered a handsome feature.

In one corner lay the glittering Crystal Maiden in silent repose. A thousand years ago, a noble girl in her early twenties was struck with a stone ax as a sacrifice to the twelve Lords of Xibalba in a desperate bid for relief from the famine. Over centuries, the waters of the gurgling creek have washed minerals over the Maiden, causing an eerie glitter to manifest from her bones.

Elsewhere, large jars collected ceremonial waters; from the stalactites dripped only the purest of pure water. Pots were ritually shattered to release spirits to appease gods who might smite the clouds to usher in the promise of rain. From blood heated in jars, stifling smoke billowed towards the mouth of the cave, wafting into azure skies.

Was the drought so unendurable so as to drive the Maya to this dreadful quest? Did the formidable Lords of Xibalba reward these lands with a generous downpour after these bloody rituals? What stark thoughts ran through the mind of the Crystal Maiden as she lay on the flowstone bed awaiting her end?

As has the powerful Maya empire itself, these secrets have mysteriously vanished. The brutal Spanish conquest in the 1500s brought an old civilization to its knees, and most codices that shed light on this ancient culture were destroyed. Only the glimmering stalagmites in front of me could provide evidence to those scenes of an ancient past.

As we turned back the way we started this thrilling exploration, I realized our

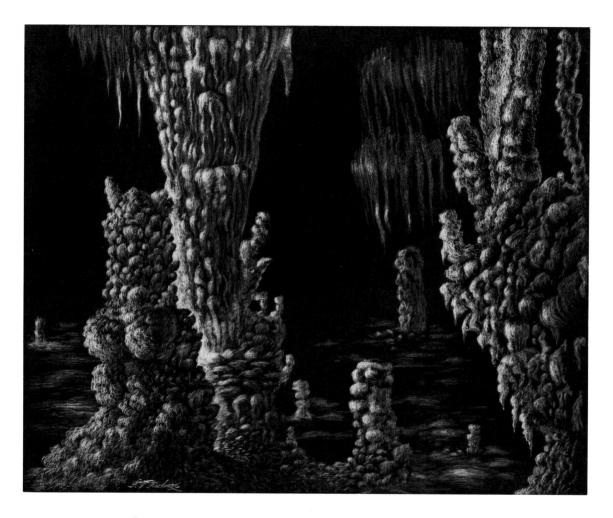

Shimmering Splendor: Giants of the Cathedral

Scratchboard and ink, 9 x 12

Beyond the artifacts of doom and death, I swam and scrambled past jagged ledges into a vast chamber. This was an immense world of heart-stopping majesty. Droplets of water glistened on the stalactites. Popcorn formations stood up to the curtained backdrop of eerie flowstones. Weird shapes rose up from the floor against the gleam of my headlamp, lending some life and sparkle to the somber history of this place. ❖ We all stood still in silent awe. ❖ No medium could capture the essence of this powerful moment as well as a scratchboard could. But I wasn't satisfied with a black and white product—the vigor of nature's dance was missing. I used a coat of yellow, brown, and orange to accentuate the effect of light setting fire to the rocks.

Oh, What a Horrific End!:
Sacrificial Remains by the Flowstone Monoliths

Watercolor, 11 x 14

Many caves present a speleological spectacle to the unsuspecting adventurer, sparkling with intricate calcite formations: stalagmites kissing stalactites in slender columns and translucent flowstones with a thousand delicate folds glimmering in the light from some unnatural source. ❖ Bleeding and tired of scrambling among jagged rocks, I clambered up a slippery boulder and witnessed this splendid sight. Along with it on the ground were scattered human skulls and sacrificial remains and my son, crouching to take a careful look at something that caught his attention. ❖ My artist's imagination triggered off a series of horrific visual possibilities I simply could not banish. I imagined the head priest swinging his blunt ax upon an unsuspecting victim with suddenness, snuffing out a life in the hope of a divine benediction. The braver victims may have known what was coming and may have graciously submitted themselves to their destiny that would redeem the living. ❖ At this point, Orlando had handed us our cameras, and I snapped away a few pictures. I used several washes of watercolor to portray this scene of mystery and horror.

adventure was about to come to an end. I carefully retraced my steps, emerging at last into the welcome brilliance of the afternoon sunlight (pages 30-1). Three hours in a dark embrace had strangely transformed me, taking me into a time unknown. As I stepped into the beautiful sights and sounds of the present moment, I was thankful for the simplest of things I had returned to.

I knew I would never forget my hair-raising tryst with a forgotten past. ❖

Beauty in the Wild: Brazilian Red Cloak

Colored pencil, 14 x 11

Some time after experiencing that rush of adrenaline, I sat down by a clearing in Teakettle Village, waiting for the bus to take me and my family back to the hotel. By this time, I was eager for anything soothing and delicate to distract me; something more calming than death and drought. ❖ *As I sat upon a large boulder, my wife, Ramaa, espied this shrub laden with lovely red flowers in full blossom. Orlando quickly transformed into an erudite botanist and identified this as the herbaceous, fast growing Brazilian Red Cloak that is very common in these parts.* ❖ *I spotted a few ladybugs walking with purpose up and down the stalk. Then, I put the colored pencils in my backpack to good effect.*

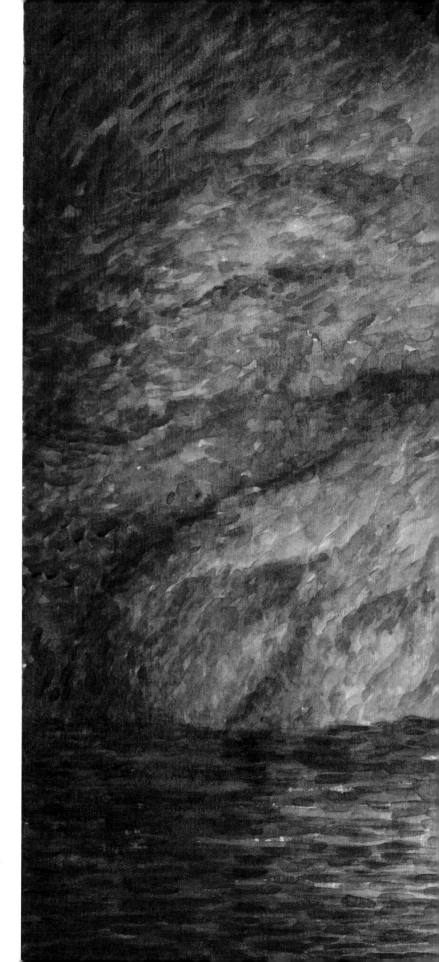

End of an Adventure: Welcome Back to the Human World!

Watercolor, 11 x 14

This cave had transformed me with the magic of its dark embrace. As our tour group stumbled into the welcome gleam of sunlight, I was simply glad to be alive. ❖ The splash of colors above the ground startled my senses. Through the gourd-shaped cave entrance I could tell that the sun was on its way down and had set the skies ablaze. I saw two men whooping for joy, taking in the joyous sight before them — a stark contrast to the murkiness and death they had just left behind. ❖ Having no paper or paint, I could only make a mental note of the scene, and later recreated it from memory.

Clink of Anklets: Apsara Lintel, Hall of the Dancers, Preah Khan

Graphite on paper, 18 x 14

The tradition of the long-lost apsara dancers fascinates me. Named after the celestial artistes of Hindu mythology, hundreds of these damsels over the generations have dedicated their lives to dancing in the temples of Angkor as an act of devotion to the gods enshrined there. ❖ As I walked along the stone rubble of Preah Khan, I came upon the Hall of the Dancers. I could imagine a scene from a thousand years ago enacted in this stony courtyard. Comely apsaras bedecked in jewelry and tiaras would be readying themselves for yet another performance, waiting for the king to arrive with his ministerial retinue. The halls would have reverberated with song and beat, the clink of anklets and jeweled bangles keeping up the cadence. ❖ The apsaras are, sadly, long gone, their tradition snuffed out by war and conquests, but their memories remain frozen in the Hall of the Dancers. This lifelike apsara caught my eye; she must have been a lead, for she was surrounded by smaller, less prominent dancers. ❖ I made a graphite rendition, the dull gray tones reminding me that where was once color and life, now stood cold stone and frozen memories from a distant past.

CHAPTER TWO

CAMBODIA ❖ ANGKOR

DANCE OF THE APSARAS

Ancient prayers may be muted and countless footprints have been erased, but timeworn temple towns throb with the energy of selfless worship by the millions who have passed through their hallowed portals. As I walked into the some of the many shrines of Angkor, I was instantly mesmerized by their divine power. Over the course of just a few centuries, those kings of yore built their mythical heaven on this earth, creating one of the greatest temple complexes in the world.

The much-awaited apsara dance in the temple town of Siem Reap lit up the stage in a riot of costume and color. The deliberate lilt of the music reached a crescendo, signaling the next performance — a Khmer folk dance performed with bamboo poles.

Sadly, touristy reenactments in a buffet setting are all that can be replayed of a rich Cambodian culture that began in the early ninth century and lasted six hundred golden years before vibrant towns and awe-inspiring temples allowed vines and trees to clasp stone and sculpture in a stranglehold for centuries to follow (pages 36, 37, 44-5).

Ten centuries ago this place was part of the massive Khmer settlement of Angkor in the ancient kingdom of Kambuja. One evening I was patiently waiting for the sunset spectacle by the stony steps of Phnom Bakheng. King Yasovarman of the Khmer dynasty consecrated this mountain temple to the Hindu god Shiva, overseer of destruction. Its stony spires rose to the summit, for upon the mythical Mount Meru of the Hindu legends rested the gods in heaven. Now, as the golden orb sank down into the treetops, I pictured how more than a thousand years ago, the searing May sun would have instead descended into the bustle of Yasodharapura, the capital city of that era.

In fact, this was but one of the many great cities of that age. Sprawling more than 1,150 square miles, Angkor, meaning *city* in Khmer, was the largest settlement of those times, overshadowing even the eighty-one-square-mile Maya city of Tikal in its zenith. The famed temple of Angkor Wat (right) was just a mile away, but little known to many, this gigantic monument is only a small relic in a vast Khmer kingdom that stretched from Thailand and Laos to the Malay Peninsula and Vietnam, the entire area dotted with sacred shrines of power.

RISE OF THE GOD KINGS

Khmer history starts with the legend of Kambu Swayambhuva, an Indian prince who, ordained by a divine commandment, marched into the jungles of Indochina. Kambu defeated the Naga king and married his daughter, Mera, thus establishing regency over the vast kingdom of Funan in the Mekong delta of southern Vietnam. Given its active maritime trade with India, Funan was steeped in Indian lore and theology. Very soon, the region expanded its boundaries, becoming a powerful economic force of those times.

In the sixth century, a tributary state called Chenla revolted and took over all of Funan, and the new king Bhavavarman changed the name of this now-

5:30 A.M.: Sunrise at Angkor Wat

Watercolor, 10 x 14

I sprang from bed at 4:00 A.M. and dashed down the stairs to find my smiling guide, Hemen, and Rain, our driver, waiting by the lobby. A short ride in pitch darkness brought us to the Naga balustrade of Angkor Wat, from where we started to walk along a stone path lit up by Hemen's flashlight. We came upon a grassy patch, and I soon realized we weren't the first visitors out there. Tea vendors were doing a brisk business, and I quickly found out why. Thrown in with the tea was a free dry spot on one of the several plastic mats splayed on the soggy grass. A couple of stingy tourists who refused to pay this premium soon changed their minds as they tried to pat their wet trousers dry. It had rained heavily the night before. ❖ I waited for what seemed like an hour braving the relentless onslaught of mosquitoes. A Japanese tourist caused a commotion when a large beetle disappeared into her dress and could be dislodged only by a vigorous dance that was a bit incongruous against this calm setting. ❖ I looked at my watch. It was 5:30 A.M., and a faint glint of gold kissed the skies. A minute later there was a hurrah from the crowd as the shy sun magically appeared from the loom of the spires of Angkor Wat, setting ablaze the pond with its water lilies and speckling the hyacinths in gold. ❖ The slumbering sky was now tickled by a palette of hues: violet, gray, pink, gold, and red. Everything came to a standstill for a few admiring minutes, and very soon it was just another day in Angkor.

Serpent Shock: Library, Preah Khan

Scratchboard and ink, 9 x 12

It was difficult to believe that pillage or the elements could have reduced a glorious shrine to such rubble. Almost like a Western medieval legend, the story runs that long years ago the king's sword was housed here under constant surveillance, for the person who would possess the weapon would become the monarch. ❖ As I struggled for my next foothold upon yet another granite block strewn on the ground, I caught my breath at the scene ahead of me. Verdant shoots sprang out of dark stone, glinting against the slanting sun. Blue skies lent a soothing, cool contrast in the background of lush silk cotton trees. A magnificent yaksha (nature-spirit) menacingly held a club, threatening me should I come any nearer and take over the sword and the kingdom's suzerainty. ❖ As I sat upon a stone squeezing paint I heard a rustle in the grass behind me. A snake slithered at startling speed among the stones and, jerking in alarm, I spilled my palette of contrasting hues upon my spotless beige trousers.

enlarged kingdom to Kambuja, after its founder. In the eighth century, Kambuja was subjugated by the powerful Sailendra kings of Java, but a vassal, Jayavarman II of Khmer lineage, broke away from this federation, establishing himself as the devaraja (god-king) in a grand ceremony in the year 802. Thus started six centuries of glory in Angkor.

As new rulers rose in power, each would aspire to be a mightier devaraja, a pharaoh who was God come down upon earth. From a procession of mighty kings

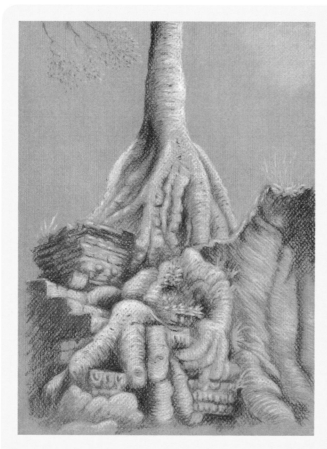

The Divine Stranglehold

Pastel on paper, 11 x 8

It was indeed a strange sight. With its fingerlike roots, the tree seemed to be clutching the shrine in an inseparable grip, even as its tentacles crawled all over the temple rooftop. As I looked closer, I realized this was more than one tree; I counted at least three trees engaged in this tussle of who gets what part of the shrine. ❖ Given the age of the rubble, it was hard telling stone apart from root; they seemed to merge into one. ❖ An allegory that Hemen, my guide, proffered didn't resound with me, for this surely didn't seem like the legendary fight between the gods and the demons, a scene plentifully depicted all across the Angkor temples. To me this was a more comely depiction of the spirit of man merging with the divine being, glorified by the ancient Khmers through poetry and stone. ❖ I used pastel on gray paper to draw out the highlights of the scene.

Watchful Eyes: Avalokiteswara Heads of Bayon

Scratchboard, 9 x 12

Many of the historical sites in Angkor were about the greatest of rulers: King Jayavarman VII, who was deified as the persona of Avalokiteswara, the god who looks down with compassion at all his subjects. ❖ Early one afternoon, after passing a herd of tourists on elephantback, my guide and I entered the southern gate of Angkor Thom, the last capital of this great empire. We stopped to take pictures of what I thought was an interesting structure; I could see four faces atop the gate. ❖ "Wait until we get to Bayon," Hemen, my guide, chuckled. ❖ Only much later, after I had climbed up into the temple of Bayon, was I truly struck by the uniqueness of it all. From a distance, the structure could have been a big clump of gray stone. But walking along the passages, I realized that the ancient king, in groupings of four faces, was watching me from everywhere. From every lintel, looming upon every spire, through every window, there he was, four faces smiling benignly, eyes shut in deep contemplation of the divine. Even more interesting was the fact that each of the 216 faces were unique; not one looked like another. ❖ The gray skies threatened impending rain and did little to brighten up the stones, so I decided to go with a scratchboard to light up the drawing with those smiling faces. I then used my stylus to capture the detail of the intricate stonework.

that followed in succession, two are notable: Suryavarman II, the grand builder of Angkor Wat, and Jayavarman VII, the most popular Khmer king of all time. The latter monarch built some of the largest temples and reservoirs, and most importantly, like Avalokiteswara, the god of compassion that he emulated, he built more than a hundred hospitals to tend to his people.

Standing by the South Gate of Angkor Thom, the capital city of Jayavarman VII, I couldn't miss the unmistakable confluence of religions here. Four huge heads of Avalokiteswara (left) smiled down upon an array of stone devas and asuras (gods and demons) engaged in the act of churning the ocean in their quest for immortality. As if in doubt, the kingdom alternated between the worship of Shiva, the Hindu overseer of destruction, and Vishnu, the Hindu god of protection, until Buddhism gained dominance. With Sukhothai and Ayutthaya becoming centers of power in neighboring Thailand, emboldened Thais pillaged Angkor in 1431, beginning the decline of a great civilization.

Infrequently visited by stray traders or missionaries, the city and its shrines were lost to the world until 1860, when an intrepid French explorer, Henri Mahout, revealed his surreal account of enormous temples in impenetrable jungles.

Despite scholarly conjectures, not much is known about this ancient people. Palm-leaf manuscripts were destroyed by pillages and floods. Only the stone stelae, carved in Sanskrit and found in temple courtyards, whisper secrets from a bygone era.

The most reliable account comes from a Chinese diplomat, Zhou Daguan, who spent a year in the court of King Srindravarman in 1296, documenting the lives of those times. His account talks of Brahmin priests and consecrations, a majestic royal court and celebrations. While temples were built of stone, noblemen lived in luxurious wooden houses, and the common gentry lived in thatched huts upon stilts to protect themselves from the floods. Palace halls came alive with the dance worship of hundreds of apsara maidens, a sacred art handed down through the generations. Kings played a key role in facilitating the harvest of rice, building massive irrigation reservoirs or barays, some as enormous as the West Baray, a tank that could hold almost two billion cubic feet of water.

Hemen, my guide, had a different explanation. The king was deified as god on earth, extending his divine rule over Angkor. He was seated atop Mount Meru and the baray was symbolic of the milky oceans surrounding this holy mountain in the Hindu mythological cosmos.

It was a transformational experience as I walked the long causeway and the snake balustrades of Angkor Wat, a moment I had awaited for many years. As a cool breeze swept the lily ponds into a ripple, I felt very much like a pilgrim of those times taking hurried steps to witness a grand story of the Hindu epics retold in stone, patiently and in eye-catching detail. I was ready to lose myself in the labyrinth of walkways, grand galleries of art, and wonders of architecture that kings of yore would have inaugurated to the boom of fireworks and the clink of apsara anklets. I was preparing to be with divinities and kings.

Built by Suryavarman II in the early twelfth century, Angkor Wat had taken more than three decades and over fifty thousand men to construct. Thirty-seven steps were built on the face of the last spire, as many as needed to climb to the legendary heavens of the Hindus. Here was once housed a golden image of Vishnu seated on his avian vehicle, Garuda. An active Buddhist monastery today, huge stone images of the Buddha looked down from sanctums facing each cardinal direction.

Intricately carved devatas (female divinities) vie with apsaras for space upon the massive walls by the slender stone balusters of the temple. Sprawling in a two-hundred-acre complex with several galleries featuring massive bas-reliefs from Hindu mythology and scenes from daily life, charming Angkor Wat recounts through stone the stories of times gone by.

It was easy to transport myself to a different era, imagining ancient masons chipping away at sandstone and laterite, creating places of eternity. Brahmin priests poured their oblations to the sivalingas, the stone emblems of the god Shiva watched over by their god-king in reverential worship. Apsaras danced as the prayers reached a crescendo. Fireworks lit up the sky during the New Year, while the ruler in his royal finery watched the pageantry from the Terrace of the Leper King.

Souvenir Girl: Glorious Brick Shrines of Pre-Rup

Pen and ink on paper, 14 x 18

Climbing up the steps of Pre-Rup was an exhilarating experience. After ascending the narrow steps to the Khmer heavens, I could look at the distant majesty of Angkor Wat. A spectacular shrine of crumbling brick, this was one of the few temples from the top of which I could command a 360-degree view of the Angkor landscape. ❖ I felt the exhilaration of a Khmer king as I sat upon a ledge all by myself, feeling the dry afternoon breeze sweep back my hair. Very soon I encountered a little girl who had followed me to the top; she was selling typical Cambodian souvenirs: birds and butterflies shaped by plastic strands tightly intertwined basket-style and held up by a string. She too seemed enthralled by the scene; forgetting her business, she joined me in staring at the vast array of ancient brick pyramids against the backdrop of the azure skies and the sprinkle of human activity below. ❖ I used pen for my drawing in order to capture all the intricate elements of the brick-by-brick theme. Only an ink wash could preserve the brilliance of the hues all around me.

Havens of the Devout

The Bayon Temple, built by Jayavarman VII, is a vast Buddhist complex with over two hundred huge Avalokiteswara heads smiling benevolently from their lofty perches.

Another Shiva temple, ancient Pre-Rup (page 41), meaning "turn the body," was built in 961 and remains a mystery. As I watched the five ruddy towers of brick and laterite gleaming in the sunlight, I wondered how a hallowed place of worship could turn into a crematorium where ashes were scattered to the winds as the funeral rites progressed.

I later walked into what was once King Jayavarman VII's Buddhist monastery of Banteay Kdei, the Citadel of Chambers. Here was an array of stone cells where monks of yore would have meditated in lone prayer, congregating in the hall for worship.

Do Not Disturb: Deity, Ta Prohm

Ink on paper, 10 x 14

I wouldn't have noticed this shy divinity hiding in the roots had it not been for a mouse that scurried into a thicket. After a scary rendezvous with a serpent the day before, I was now vigilant in looking for snakes as well as for landmines. I made a point of looking out for trouble on the ground as I lugged my art paraphernalia around with me. ❖ All over the terrain, the spung trees had made their conquest, covering shrine and stone with their long tentacles. ❖ Hemen, my guide, had gone on ahead, looking for bigger vistas I could capture on paper. I trailed behind, taking in the antiquity of it all. As I followed the startled mouse with my eyes, I noticed a deity playing hide-and-seek with me in a corner unlit by the flash of the camera and unknown to the guidebook circuit. Even in the darkness I could make out that benign smile of meditative bliss. ❖ Maybe it wanted to be left alone in its divine contemplations. ❖ A wispy wash of ink was enough. The rest was left to the imagination of the viewer.

Not far away is the much-pictured temple of Ta Prohm, or "Old Brahma." This Buddhist monastery has been popularized by the Tomb Raider sequence filmed here. The shrine was dedicated to Prajnaparamita, the Buddhist personification of wisdom, and the central image was modeled after the king's mother. It was an otherworldly sight in the midst of the jungle, with gigantic silk cotton trees gripping stone and sculpture. Most of Angkor would have looked like this when it was rediscovered in the mid-1800s.

A forty-five-minute drive took me to a tenth-century Khmer jewel with its delicate carvings in red sandstone: the Banteay Srei, the "Citadel of Women." An astounding masterpiece conceived by a minister of the royal court, this majestic temple glimmered with reliefs from Hindu mythology. Indra, god of the celestial beings, resplendently rides Airavata, his elephantine mount on a pediment, while nearby on a lintel the god Krishna tussles with a demon. Two libraries stand in silence; once upon a time, thousands of palm-leaf manuscripts must have filled the stone shelves inside.

I walked in these sacred lands with my guide for almost three days, sunrise to sunset, and explored only a sliver of the vastness of the Khmer empire.

An Era Ended

High up in a balloon late one afternoon, I looked down at the ancient city and its vast stretch of shrines and rice fields. The hill temple of Phnom Bakheng looked very different from far away. The vastness of Angkor Wat was only now apparent; its large causeway and the oceans that surrounded the divine Mount Meru transforming an earthly city to a realm of the gods.

Everywhere in Angkor, mysteries abound and questions remain unanswered. Does Angkor Wat face west because it was a funerary memorial? When did the apsara damsels and their tradition come to an end? Why was the god of death worshiped in the Terrace of the Leper King? Why did the Brahmin Kambu set out upon his conquest?

Only the god-kings of yore and their wise counselors know the answers to these questions. ❖

Too Close for Comfort: Spung Tree at Ta Prohm

Acrylic on paper, 16 x 20

Could I have traveled back to a time when the French explorer Henri Mahout excitedly stumbled upon the tree-strangled landscape of Angkor? ❖ Everywhere I looked, I saw tall silk cotton trees holding the secrets of ancient shrines in a viselike grip, just as they had for decades. Their roots seemed to have a life of their own as they reached out to anything that stood still. ❖ In front of me loomed this lone majesty, its gleaming roots caressing the mossy roof of an ancient temple, while its bolder ones were set upon an exploration into the hallway of the shrine. Tireless green shoots fought their way out of stone and shade, breaking the monotony of this setting. ❖ A dainty apsara figurine watched me from her stony perch, lending an element of softness to the drama. ❖ I had to capture all this in a quick sketch and twenty clicks of the camera before the next tourist discovered my secret.

Tryst of the Sisters: Pele Meets Nāmaka

Acrylic on paper, 12 x 16

Armed with seismological models and fancy-looking contour charts, volcanologists emphatically tell you that Pele doesn't meet her adversarial sister Nāmaka these days. Speaking in more scientific terms, they'll describe how fiery lava flows sluggishly into private land in Kalapana only to come to a stop, no longer trickling down to the waters of the Pacific Ocean. ❖ It was around 9:00 P.M. as I floundered upon the sharp rocks, struggling to keep my balance upon the hardened volcanic floor. I walked behind our rather quiet guide, Steve, flashlight in tow. From a point ahead, I could hear a hiss as lava strayed from its path just a little bit, wrapping another helpless tree in a final embrace. ❖ If this scene was so awesome, what would that meeting between lava and the ocean, Pele and Nāmaka, look like? Sisters in conflict, encountering one another after a long separation would mean a powerfully emotional embrace of the opposites. Flecks of lava would light up the foam even as the goddess would touch down into the waters in a powerful surge. ❖ Earlier I saw some fascinating pictures clicked by a couple of daredevil photographers who had the temerity to swim in 110-degree waters; that was as far as they could get since getting a bit closer to the lava flow would certainly have killed them. Pele would wield her O'o stick like a brush, much like a consummate artist, using lava as her paint and her sister as a vast canvas. ❖ I felt thwarted that I wouldn't be able to witness this reunion that day, so I recreated such a scene from maybe more than a decade ago using my imagination.

CHAPTER THREE

UNITED STATES OF AMERICA ❖ HAWAII

FUMES AND FURY: IN PELE'S PLAYGROUND

The unbridled power of raw nature was awe-inspiring. Below the twinkling stars, I could see the sacred fire pit where the restless goddess Pele was astir. Volcanic fumes glowed orange and yellow, hissing in contained rage. Deep down in the caldera was gurgling lava.

All of a sudden there would come that spectacular moment when the fiery goddess would emerge, clad in golden robes, wreaking destruction upon the old with the promise of the new.

The hush of the night was broken only by the growls from the fiery cauldron. I stood under the stars upon the Jaggar Museum Overlook, gazing at one of the world's most sacred sites, marked only by nature's unbridled fury. It is believed that here, within the deep bowels of the Halema'uma'u Crater, Pele, the Polynesian goddess of volcanoes, fire, and lightning, maintains her earthly abode.

Pele's kingdom encompasses the Kilauea volcano, of which the crater is but a small part. The poetic imagery of Hawaiian legends recounts how when she shakes her matted tresses loose, the Pu'u 'O'o vent (page 50) screams out to the skies, billowing thick sulfurous smoke. The steaming flues blur the landscape with vapor heated by magma that flows but a couple of hundred feet underneath. Several craters from recent eruptions and wide rift zones dot this barren landscape.

One of the world's youngest and most active volcanoes, Kilauea on Hawaii's Big Island, has been raging for only 300,000 years, unlike the older sleeping Mauna Loa, which looms nearby. The Pacific tectonic plate, which lies under the Hawaiian chain of islands, has been moving above a hotspot, creating a chain of volcanoes for hundreds of thousands of years.

Pele's journey takes her wherever the magma flows. Known as the Big Island or simply as Hawaii, the southernmost of the Hawaiian islands is home to five such volcanoes. Kilauea awoke from slumber in 1983, but the now dormant Mauna Loa and Hualalai are just taking a brief rest.

Mountains of Fire

One sunny morning, I left the beaches of Kona on the western leeward side of the island, driving past the lush Waipi'o Valley and the desert ecosystem of Waimea into the bustling town of Hilo. Less than a hundred years ago, molten lava surged into the outskirts of this town, threatening to bring waste and devastation.

Thirty miles from Hilo and a couple of miles from the Hawaii Volcanoes National Park lies the quiet village of Volcano. Here the ever-present smell of vog, a real word for volcanic smog, adds a curtain of mystery to these hills of fire. Vents exhale scorching vapor through holes on the plains, billowing smoke in columns of wispy white. Yellowed rocks plastered with sulfurous fumes fleck the terrain. Black boulders lie scattered all over the ground, remnants of several eruptions over the years.

Along what is known as the Crater Rim Drive, Pele's power of destruction is all too apparent. A short walk from the parking lot of the Kilauea Overlook led

10:00 P.M.: View from Jaggar Museum Overlook

Pastel on board, 10 x 12

I visited the Jaggar Museum early one morning. Seismographs and blinking contraptions seemed to be in complete control. A local scientist was leading a group of camera-toting Japanese tourists; his fervent geological narrative to me sounded like arcane mumbo jumbo. ❖ I returned later that night, though I was very tired after several long hours of hiking. Our volcano expert, Arthur, insisted on a final stop before we called it a day and I had grudgingly agreed. ❖ The museum's parking lot was a hive of activity as we crossed the lane over to the lookout. I stood hypnotized by the sight that greeted me. ❖ Tourists watched in amazement as an orange glow flicked in that dark night under the stars. A pink hue tinged the clouds above the raging caldera that was Pele's playground. A lone tree, a helplessly rooted captive, faced the caldera, licked by flecks of gold and red. ❖ There was a certain mystique to the scene that I felt was best left to the viewer's imagination to complete. A hint of pastel on black pastel board did justice to this subject. This way I could let the strokes of pastel sticks merge with the black background, putting the focus on Pele's raging energy in the darkness of the night.

to the smoking facade of the caldera. One of the most active volcanoes in the world today, Kilauea's caldera houses the sacred firepit of Halema'uma'u (above and pages 52-3), the house of the ama'um'au fern. Legend has it that Pele once had an argument with the rain god Kamapua'a, who, angered by Pele's power to erupt at will, covered the crater with fronds of this fern. Smoked out, Pele realized the impotence of fire over water, and these two powerful divinities eventually called for a ceasefire, retreating to different parts of the same island.

For the last couple of years, the eleven-mile Crater Rim Loop Drive has been closed beyond the Jaggar Museum, so I couldn't drive up to the Halema'uma'u Overlook from where one can look at the lava activity right below. In 2008, there was a massive eruption that hurled rocks and ash, devastating the parking lot; since

Fury of the Pu'u 'O'o Vent

Scratchboard and ink, 8 x 10

Doors-off helicopter rides are a big thing in this part of the world. A chopper takes off from the unassuming coastline of sunny Kona and performs a much-touted "waterfall-landing feat" in a private area "where only our tour company has special permission to land." There you'll get to witness groups of boisterous tourists seated on makeshift picnic mats, laughing and joking around, sipping glasses of wine. ❖ As our helicopter later took off from between the cliffs and turned towards the volcanic zone, an eerie silence descended upon the group. Going from the destruction of Mauna Loa and then on to the smoke and fury of Pele's playground, Kilauea Caldera, everyone started in amazement at the raw power unleashed by nature. ❖ As we circled above the Pu'u O'o vent, I held on firmly at whatever bar or handhold I could grip, lest I fall off right into the crater's blazing mouth. Below me, gurgling lava splashed around, glaring orange through its "skylights," fissures on the hard lava shell. Toxic sulfurous fumes smoked uncontained from countless rifts in the terrain. Glowering embers spewed forth, scattering about in all directions, stippling the ground below in orange blotches. ❖ Whether by accident or design, we suddenly felt the helicopter shudder and teeter down before quickly recovering. Apparently unfazed, our pilot was telling us how it is possible, if you know your way, to land on a part of the lava field and walk around, actually feeling the scalding heat below you. ❖ Committing these striking moments to memory, I decided to capture this harsh landscape through a scratchboard drawing, tinting the board with inks to capture the vivid anger of orange.

then the drive and surrounding hiking trails have been closed to the public.

The day before, I saw a different perspective of the volcano from the air. Taking off on a helicopter tour from the sunny beaches of the Kohala Coast, we circled counterclockwise around the island, soon reaching the windward side that was covered in rain and clouds. Destruction and ruin was visible from the rage of Mauna Loa that had leveled houses and vegetation until the flow met the ocean in a plume of smoke. Once upon a time this was fertile land covered with a blanket of green koa and ohia trees, girdled by waterfalls.

As we approached the Kilauea caldera, we circled around the Pu'u 'O'o vent. Below us was molten lava gushing along vents visible through what are called skylights.

We could see the eerie orange glow as it rushed somewhere beneath the floor. Smoky

The Firepit of Halema'uma'u

Acrylic on paper, 12 x 16

Staying on the Big Island for several days, I treated myself to a traditional luau in Kona one evening. The place was packed to capacity and the buffet had already commenced when I arrived. The stage lit up to the brilliant performances of Samoan fire-knife dancers and a Tahitian troupe. ❖ Next was the hula rendition of the goddess Pele and her mystic Polynesian origins. I was simply enthralled, as the narrator proceeded to recount the legends of these parts. ❖ To me, Pele, with her fearsome tresses and her penchant for bringing creation out of destruction, seems to bear a strange similarity to the goddess Kali of Hindu mythology or the fearsome Guayota who abides in the Teide volcano in the Canary Islands. These celestial archetypes destroy so they may create. ❖ The storyteller continued his gripping tale of Pele and her sporadic appearances as an old woman with a small white dog in her magic kingdom, which is the Big Island. ❖ Early the next morning, fog enveloped the park in its secret embrace. As I took in the powerful scene by the Halema'uma'u Crater I was still intrigued by the story I had heard the night before. A Hawaiian family came by with offerings of leis, reverentially placing them upon the holy terrain where the goddess dwelt. An old woman moved into the foreground, wanting to take a closer look. ❖ I watched the orange glow from within the churning caldera; the goddess seemed restlessly eager to accept the gifts. The ground was pockmarked with smoky exhalations from the depths of the earth where Pele moved around in restive rage. A lone tree seemed to cling upon a precarious slope where it had stubbornly taken root. I now imagined the old woman with her dog and fearsome O'o stick, which when struck would unleash divine destruction of the old, bringing in the new. ❖ This was indeed an elevating moment for me. I created an acrylic portrayal of the legend and profound symbolism of such a theme.

Lava Ladies: Nene Mother and Gosling

Scratchboard, 12 x 16

Late one evening, I took a bus to Kalapana; soon I would be walking atop harsh lava fields that can cut through shoes if you don't watch your step carefully, or worse still, leave you with gashes or stitches if you trip and lose your balance. ❖ *I looked at the silvery clouds above on a moonlit night, just a day shy of a full orb in the sky. As I blundered forward with my flashlight I came upon this sight not far from the ocean. A mother nene was gushing over her gosling, which seemed to be nonchalantly waddling its way through jagged stones.* ❖ *I don't think they took notice of me as I studied them from behind a rocky outcrop, noting details lit up by bold moonlight. Extant only in this part of the world, the nene, or the Hawaiian goose, seemed a lot more regal in bearing than its commonly seen cousins around the world.* ❖ *I decided to work this night scene on scratchboard, since this medium seemed the most apt for my subject. I chose not to color my work of art since the contrast between soft plumage against harsh rock was best depicted with more emphasis by simply leaving my scratchboard in its original form.*

exhalations rose up in the gray terrain, as water and brimstone breathed out the vents with a hiss. A few years ago, Pele would have rushed down to the sea to meet her legendary sister Nāmaka, Princess of the Ocean, but this is an unpredictable event and hasn't happened in a while. Today one can witness volcanic lava flowing down slowly through what is private property in the town of Kalapana.

The Chain of Craters Road is a twenty-mile paved roadway located in the park that passes along ancient craters, dormant lava flows, and views of the tropical rainforests as the seacoast glimmers far ahead. Early in the drive, I stopped to see the stark lava trees left standing after a rush of lava had encased the vegetation, eating away the insides within the bark. Soon I reached Mauna Ulu, a crater formed as Kilauea erupted again, starting in 1969 with a forceful gush of molten rock that closed the Chain of Craters Road. Some of the fountains soared to over one thousand feet high in a dazzling display of light and color. Interestingly, over five years of eruption added more than two hundred acres to the coastline.

Hiking through Destruction

The Kilauea Iki Overlook stares down upon a desolate wasteland. More than fifty years ago, a rift yawned open, exploding nineteen hundred feet of furious brimstone into the skies, leaving a churning sea of lava and waves of molten rock lapping against tall cliffs. The six-mile hike along the Kilauea Iki Trail took me to the innards of volcanic power. I continued hiking through lush rainforest and past giant ferns in search of the reclusive happy-face spider, so named for the funny sign on its body.

In this lush tropical forest, red lehua blossoms adorned the ohia trees. The rainforest soon descended to the now-hardened lava lake, which still smoldered in patches. Fiery magma was but 250 feet below me. Scrambling among rocks, I reached the now pacified vent — the Pu'u Pua'i cinder cone, from where the calamity had erupted. It was hard to imagine that the same dry landscape that I stood on was only recently churning with red lava. Harder still to believe is that just a few hundred years from now, tall trees and giant ferns will likely cover this very terrain. Pele's forceful transformation of destruction and creation is but a magic of contradictions.

Even in milliseconds of cataclysmic outburst, Pele, the eternal sculptress, would create a work of art on this black canvas. I noticed glistening droplets of lava, sometimes called Pele's tears, scattered all around me. Green specks of peridot glimmered in the slanting sunlight. A'a lava puckered with holes splattered all over, while the pahoehoe lava presented itself in undulating folds, much like black drapery that stretched as far as the eye could see. Irresistibly exotic as they looked, I didn't dare pocket any rocky souvenirs. Hawaiians believe that these lava rocks are possessed by strange spirits and that Pele treats them as her own progeny; misfortune befalls the hapless one who steals from her playground.

The legend of sacred Pele lives on in these parts. Witnesses narrate sightings of an old woman who walks these desolate grounds with a white dog, begging for food. She bestows riches and good fortune on the generous, cursing the parsimonious. She wreaks her anger on the ones who turn their backs to her.

The locals loved telling me the story of the late nineteenth-century Princess Ruth Keelikoani, who having converted to Christianity decided to decry such superstition. In an act of defiance she traveled to the crater, hurling invectives and throwing rocks into the caldera. Soon thereafter the rage of the goddess was let loose. When Kilauea erupted and the lava flow gurgled towards populous Hilo, the princess was summoned to appease Pele's anger. It is said that when she made her votive offerings of silk scarves and alcoholic spirits, the flow stopped.

It was evening as I climbed back through the cliffs up above the lava bed, back onto the forest trail above. I wondered how this trail would have looked with smoldering lava churning below amid the hiss and boom of nature's cacophony.

The parking lot at the Jaggar Museum was busy that night. Named after an intrepid volcanologist from Boston, seismographs here measure the faintest rumble across several craters from miles away; from those broad scratches on the paper drum, Kilauea seemed the most restless.

Lazy Ladybugs: Lehua Blossom

Pastel, 10 x 8

I engaged a tour company to lead us along the Kilauea Iki Trail. Arthur, my guide, was narrating the story of the lehua blossom. Belief goes that the goddess Pele was once smitten by a handsome man named Ohia who was engaged to a girl named Lehua. When Ohia refused to abandon Lehua, the angry goddess turned him into a tree. Taking pity on the young girl, the gods watching this drama from the heavens transformed Lehua into a flower upon that very tree, uniting the lovers for eternity. Hawaiians believe that when this sacred flower is plucked from the tree, the heavens rain down tears evoked by the sorrow of separation. ❖ *Lehua blossoms come in orange, yellow and red. My children, Anish and Amrita, were set on spotting a happy-face spider in its web. As we continued walking along the Kilauea Iki Trail, we came across a gaggle of nene picking at berries. Dappled sunlight was falling on a patch of ohia trees. Blood-red lehua blossoms splayed out from everywhere in the thicket.* ❖ *The softness of the flower and the rutbbery texture of its sentinel leaves were best captured in a quick pastel drawing. I used a softer cold-pressed paper to render the texture of one of one the big island's favorite legends.*

Despite all the blinking gadgets and newfangled contraptions, the whims of Pele cannot be contained. Clad in fiery red robes, the goddess of volcanoes will one day awake, destroy, and then recreate, as she has always been doing over the centuries in her frisky cadence. ❖

Fire and Smoke, the End of It All: Manikarnika Ghat

Arylic on hardboard, 16 x 20

Varanasi crudely brings the truth home. It took me a while to absorb the stark reality of the end of human existence. For the first few days of my trip, I fearfully avoided this area, climbing up to the lanes and descending a few ghats away from the burning pyres. Here, bodies were lined up in preparation for eternal salvation, while the dom, the officiator, mechanically went about his chore of organizing the rites. ❖ One day, emboldened by the nonchalance all around me, I took some time to observe the whole scene and found myself mesmerized by its darkly captive magic. I looked past the somber flames that shot up the wood pyre and saw the temple spires and watchtowers ominously gazing down upon this landscape as they have done for centuries. ❖ For the living, life moved on, just as it does everywhere. Children were flying kites, laughing. Women laden with baskets of flowers on their heads were headed for worship at a nearby shrine. Boatmen lay in wait to ferry the next load of passengers, one fixing a plank that had fallen loose. The four-legged menagerie of dogs, goats, buffalos, donkeys, and cows were making the usual nuisance of themselves. ❖ I sketched this "another day in the life" scene in about fifteen minutes, using color pencil to capture the interplay of light and shade. Later I completed an acrylic painting on hardboard that I prepared myself.

CHAPTER FOUR

INDIA ❖ VARANASI

DANCING TO THE DRUMBEAT: IN SHIVA'S KINGDOM

I was indeed in a land of contradictions. Here, what would be sacrilege seemed rather sacred. Hindus thrive alongside Buddhists and Jains. Sacred chants waft to the clang of bells in the breeze that ruffle the Ganges even as funeral pyres, otherwise shunned as unholy, hungrily consume the dead near hallowed shrines.

I was in Shiva's kingdom — Varanasi, the City of Light, where sinners have been transformed into saints, where the demure Ganges washes away the horridly impure to reveal pristine goodness.

This is the holy kingdom of Shiva, where this divine caretaker watches over his citizens. In this city known as the "Great Cremation Ground," he destroys Time in order to transport both the living and dead to a luminous beyond, forever liberating them from the interminable cycle of earthly strife.

Here Shiva whispers a secret mantra in the dead man's ears, ensuring eternal salvation," Mohan, our boatman, told us, heaving his oars against the swift current. Far away from his highland abode in the misty Himalayan mountains, this Hindu god rules over the age-old city of Varanasi, a land of inconsistencies.

A full moon was rising as the sounds of clanging bells and prayer fluted in the breeze. The flames of Manikarnika Ghat (left) roared hungrily, reducing the unending train of human

The Umbrella Parade

Scratchboard, 12 x 16

One evening my extended family of fourteen took a boat ride along the Ganges. It was early evening, and the restless moon had already made itself known in the skies. ❖ Our boatman was a talkative fellow who whisked us away from a temple and proceeded to regale us with stories in his accented Hindi. ❖ We neared the loom of Dasashwamedha Ghat and into a soul-stirring moment. Distant bells were tinkling in prayer. The faraway chatter of pilgrims wafted in the evening breeze. Votive offerings of clay lamps glittered in the river, mocking the stars above. Hundreds of umbrellas were arrayed on the stone steps, lending contrast to the towering temple spires. ❖ The glistening Ganges was mirroring all that was happening. ❖ I captured this magical moment in a photograph and recreated the scene in scratchboard.

bodies to ashes, transporting souls to a heaven from which the Hindus believe there is no return. Here come the aged faithful in their sunset years, for death in Varanasi means sure moksha, a transcendental liberation from the circle of life and death.

Mohan only plies the boat here in the Ganges and readily confesses to his ignorance of the Hindu sacred texts. Such knowledge is the calling of the pandas, the priests who gather on the stone steps and in the countless temples in this City of Light. Ramdev Shastri, a priest in the Durga temple, revealed to me that Shiva's secret mantra is but the name of the god Rama, the "ideal man" incarnation of the god Vishnu.

"Brahma creates, Vishnu preserves, but Shiva destroys." This is how the priest described the Hindu trinity of gods, chewing as he did so the famous Banarsi betel-nut leaf laden with a potent mixture of spices. (A shopkeeper later conspiratorially revealed to me the secret formula of the Banarsi paan "handed down from my great grandfather": betel-nut slivers, clove, cardamom, and nutmeg, dry coconut, fennel seeds, sugar, camphor, menthol powder, and "one more thing." He wouldn't divulge the last ingredient or the specific proportions of each one!) The priest went on: "Shiva destroys the bad, the ignorance, so that knowledge and enlightenment may dawn."

Among Hinduism's seven holy cities, Varanasi, also known as Benares or Kasi, is the most ancient. Kasi means "illumination." It is verily the City of Light. Paradoxically, in this holiest of the holies, sanctity and sacrilege magically coexist. Similar to Jerusalem, sacredness and sects know no boundaries; Hindus coexist with Jains, Buddhists, and Muslims. In and around this city of learning and knowledge, the Buddha preached his sermons, the eremite Mahavira walked upholding the tenets of Jainism, and the mystic poet Kabir composed his occult verses. It is here that the inimitable philosopher Sankaracharya propounded the oneness of God and the sage Madhvacharya extolled his teachings of dualism. Land of opposites — here the dead and the living commingle nonchalantly just as do purity and dirt, all washed by the pristine sweep of the Ganges.

It was late at night when my extended family of parents, aunts, cousins, and siblings set out to the train station from a dusty Mumbai suburb for a twenty-

A Surprise Guest

Watercolor, 11 x 14

I came upon a clearing near a food stall by Lalita Ghat. Here I saw an unusual scene enacted, one that was far more likely to be set in the sands of Jaipur or Jaisalmer in Rajasthan. ❖ For sure, I didn't expect to find a camel in the bustle of the Varanasi lanes! ❖ The cart was adorned with colorful decorations and silken drapes. However, the owner was nowhere to be seen. The camel ignored the passersby as it continued to chew and stare vacantly ahead, maybe even posing for a sketch? ❖ A few minutes later Babu, the keeper, made his appearance. He had embarked on a pilgrimage all the way from Pushkar in remembrance of his parents and was offering rides to make some money while he was in town. ❖ I later completed this drawing with watercolor highlights using a dry-brush technique.

four-hour journey to the Varanasi station. My grandfather had passed on, with the parting wish that his first-year anniversary rituals be performed upon the ghats of the Ganges: embankments glittering with shops, umbrellas, animals, priests, athletes, and pilgrims, that lead down a long flight of stone steps skirting the river. My parents would need to perform a series of rituals in this "Great Cremation Ground," concluding the ceremonies with special worship in the major shrines along the Ganges.

One early morning during my two-week stay in Varanasi, I rushed from my accommodations at Kedar Ghat (pages 74-5) to watch the sunrise. I stood captivated, gazing at the three-mile sweep of the ghats that face the swath of the Ganges and the rising sun.

The river flows north from the southernmost Assi Ghat all the way to Varana Ghat; hence the name "Varanasi," which morphed into the anglicized "Benares," or, as it is also known, simply the sacred city of Kasi. Just like the ancient cities of Megiddo or Babylon, this bustling place has seen the walk of civilizations, faiths, wars, and strife, pillages and renaissance.

"Possibly inhabited by tribes from the twelfth century B.C.E.," the priest remarked, "this city is probably older than Beijing, Athens, or Jerusalem."

The resilience of this ancient city is truly amazing. Afghans, Persians, and Mughals invaded this city time and again, not so much to plunder and loot as to destroy the backbone of an unrelenting faith. Hundreds of temples were razed to the ground, sanctums desecrated, idols mutilated, but the faithful kept building. When temple turned into mosque, another would spring up elsewhere, and over time that shrine would build a reputation in its own right.

As I threaded through the winding lanes, I jostled my way past sadhus or holy men, beggars, pilgrims, cattle, and food stalls. In a city of over two thousand temples and countless small shrines, religion is all-

Peacock by a Tea Stall

Scratchboard, 8 x 6

The national bird of India is not a very common sight in this holy city, but you do occasionally see a stray one bandying its plumage around. Peacocks are considered holy, since the playful god Krishna sports a peacock feather amidst his tresses. ❖ I saw this bird eyeing me curiously by a Banarsi tea stall near Scindia Ghat. Zoological classifications aside, what struck me was how much this resplendent bird really resembles the humbler chicken at close quarters. ❖ I used a scratchboard to capture details, particularly the beak, the crinkly skin, and the bluish-green tufts of feather around its neck. I layered several washes of ink to capture the translucence of its colors.

pervasive, just like the beat of Shiva's drum. As the saying goes, in Varanasi there is no place wider than a sesame seed that isn't occupied by a sivalinga — the stone shaft that symbolizes the essence of Shiva. If Shiva wasn't the god worshiped here, it would no doubt be another divinity from among the thirty-three million gods of the Hindu religion!

Holiness has always been steeped in this place as far back as its history can be traced. Hermitages and ashrams have followed in the march of time. Several thousand years ago, even before the cult of Shiva was established, before civilizations worshiped yakshas and nagas — spirits and deities of trees, ponds, and serpents from the netherworlds. The prayers of the ancient peoples continue to this day, artfully synthesized with mainstream expressions of devotion. As the Hindus maintain, God is to be truly seen in everything, everywhere.

While most of Varanasi was rebuilt in the eighteenth century by Hindu kings, its roots haven't been forgotten. Holy Kasi is indeed a city of stories and legends that transport the listener to the days when gods traversed the skies unfettered upon their divine mounts, disembarking at such holy places at will.

"Let me tell you the legend of Ganges," Ramdev Shastri offered. "For Varanasi is really about the holy river and the transformation she performs."

The story runs that once upon a time, a king out hunting with his retinue of sixty thousand sons insulted a sage who was lost in meditation. Enraged by this effrontery, the hermit cursed the king and his progeny to be reduced to ashes. Bhagiratha, one of the king's descendants, had to perform severe penances in order to bring the Ganges down to the earth, for only this holy river, that then flowed in the heavens, could redeem such a curse by descending and coursing through the ashes of his forefathers. Yet Bhagiratha was still in a predicament, as only Shiva would be able to contain the powerful onrush of the Ganges onto the planet. Responding to his prayers, Shiva agreed to stand upon Mount Kailas in the Himalayas and contain its furious descent in his matted hair.

"As Mother Ganges rushed down mirthfully," Ramdev Shastri went on, "the trident-holding god received her in his locks, trapping her there, lest she wash away the earth and mankind itself! This was the penance of Bhagiratha, and hence the Ganges is also known as 'Bhagirathi.'"

He added: "The holy waters washed away all the sins of his ancestors, and Bhagiratha ruled wisely as a king for many years. So you see, a dip in the Ganges, the river of life, redeems one for generations."

LAND OF A MILLION SHRINES

Spread out like a crescent, the ghats of Varanasi lend an ethereal view to this sacred place. Just like the bustling temples that reside upon them, ghats have their own legends. From the limpid waters of Assi Ghat where the goddess Durga had once thrown her sword down after destroying demons, to the murky waters of Varana, nearly a hundred ghats skirt the bank of the Ganges.

Pehlwan and the Sadhu

Acrylic on hardboard, 16 x 20

During the two weeks I spent in this land of contradictions, I was an object of curiosity to many a sadhu (holy man) who watched me as I wandered the ghats making my sketches — not a common sight in this part of the world. Some of them overawed me with their appearances and appurtenances, and when they congregated as a group, I felt an element of fear. One of them, known simply as Maharaj, had ashes smeared all over his body, sported matted locks, and carried a skull and trident, the insignias of the god Shiva. Another smoked a tobacco pipe and often laughingly threatened to open a basket that housed, as he put it, one of the most poisonous cobras in India; once he did open the basket, and I shrank away. They often poked fun at me and offered me questionable food. To them this unusual city slicker offered immense entertainment. ❖ One day in the late afternoon, I was expected to arrive at the ashram where my parents were performing the anniversary ritual for my grandfather. I blundered from one ghat to the other until I had wandered hopelessly far away from my destination. It had become ominously cloudy, and a downpour seemed inevitable. For a fleeting moment the sun straggled through a cloud bank, lighting up the water and silhouetting the mottle of boats ahead. Dhobis (washermen) were hurriedly pulling clothes from makeshift strings. ❖ Unmindful of the impending downpour, a glistening pehlwan (bodybuilder) was effortlessly wielding a stone mace. Just at that moment Maharaj walked by in the foreground, calm and collected. Clad in ocher robes with smeared ashes all over him, he added an elemental contrast to the scene. ❖ I had to capture this and did a quick pastel drawing on gray paper, a clever way to capture nature's changing moods. I eventually recreated the scene on hardboard painted white, using acrylic with some pointillism and dry-brush technique I found effective.

One evening I watched the evening riverbank aarti, the worship with lights, at Dasashwamedha Ghat (page 60). Mythology runs that Brahma, the God of Creation, once performed a sacrifice here to celebrate Shiva's advent to the planet. One of the oldest ghats in Varanasi, dating to thousands of years ago, it is also the holiest, teeming with sadhus and pilgrims lost in prayer and worship.

The poet Tulsidas composed his verses of the Hindu epic Ramayana while meditating at Tulsi Ghat. The tall pyres of Harischandra Ghat cannot be missed, and legend has it that King Harischandra, the practitioner of inviolable truth, once worked in the crematorium here, the gods testing his devotion to virtue. In the burning pyres of Manikarnika Ghat the flames rise up, hungrily consuming mortal bodies, ensuring moksha, liberation for the deceased. Legend has it that when Shiva was performing his dreadful dance of destruction, a bead from his earring fell into the waters here.

In this city of seemingly countless temples, I didn't know where to begin. Yet the thousands of tourists who spill out of buses onto the winding streets of Benares seem to have a clear mission. Many come out of curiosity to see where their forefathers may have trodden hundreds of years ago, risking the perils of forests, brigands, and wild animals in quest of salvation or monkhood. Some come here to perform last rites for their dear departed, firm in their conviction that there would otherwise be no rebirth thereafter. Many pilgrims arrive during the festive months when the stars and planets align into auspicious combinations, and like during the Kumbh Mela festival, the ghats burst into color and the air is filled with unsuppressed chants of devotion.

In the busy lanes of Viswanatha Gali lies the temple of Kasi Viswanatha, venerated as the guardian of the world.

"This shrine is the most visited spot in this city," Raju, my auto-rickshaw driver and self-styled guide, explained earlier in my visit.

Wracked by centuries of pillage but rebuilt by the queen Ahilyabai Holkar in the late eighteenth century, this golden temple is not easily visible from the streets. Trying to get there, I accidentally ended up at the interesting mosque of Gyanvapi (right), which had Hindu pillars on the back, the front being a typical stucco structure.

This had been the original seat of the older Viswanatha temple when the iconoclastic emperor Aurangzeb destroyed the shrine, even as a protective priest plunged into the well with the stone sivalinga. The emperor chose to not plaster the ornate pillars with stucco as a testament to his conquest over the Hindu faith.

Integration Inconceivable: Gyanvapi Mosque

Scratchboard, 12 x 16

Sepia wash, 12 x 16

Pen and ink, 16 x 20

The contradiction was startling — here was an inconceivable integration of faiths. Huge minarets and white domes in the front disguised the remains of an ancient temple behind. ❖ A ruthless Muslim emperor had razed an ancient temple to the ground and intentionally left these walls intact as a reminder of his intolerant might over other beliefs. In a fit of rage, he raided the temple's sanctum and hurled the sivalinga into the Gyan Vapi, the Well of Knowledge. ❖ As I walked along the grounds, I saw a few cows lazing around under the blazing afternoon sun, unmindful of the gory events this place must have witnessed three hundred years ago. ❖ I made an elaborate pen drawing in about forty-five minutes. ❖ A sepia wash with ink highlights seemed to be the best way to capture the softness of this scene. The past seemed long forgotten in the search for a new age of peace. ❖ I later recreated this same scene on a scratchboard to enable me to capture more details of the intricately carved walls of a temple long gone.

The Gyanvapi mosque abuts the abode of the god-king of Varanasi. Unlike at most of the elaborate temples, space here comes at a premium, and very quickly I was inside the sanctum where the idol is housed. An oblong black stone, the Lord of Kasi is worshiped here as a jyotirlinga — a symbol of effulgent light.

"Varanasi is known as the City of Light for yet another reason," Ramdev Shastri had told me. Countless years ago, when Brahma and Vishnu were contemplating the true nature of God, a blinding beam of light from below the netherworlds split the ground asunder, flaring an endless way up to the heavens. This was the essence of godhood without any earthly attributes." He then recited a Sanskrit verse and continued: "The place where this happened is right here; it was in holy Benares."

The Temple Heist

Scratchboard, 8 x 10

The rhesus monkeys, or what I simply call "temple monkeys," are a frequent sight in these parts of the world. However, the Hanuman langur is probably less common in urban areas of Varanasi. Named after the Hindu monkey-god Hanuman, these primates are treated with some reverence. ❖ It was evening in the Cowrie Mata temple, where pilgrims offer the traditional goodbye to Shiva's sister before departing the city. As I was climbing the steps, I heard a ruckus somewhere above the rocks. A hungry mother langur had made away with someone's lunch of Indian bread and curry rice and was bounding up the rocks, her baby in tow. A woman screamed at her simian adversary, waving her hands menacingly. ❖ A male langur watched this scene from a ledge above. As the sun slanted on his face, lighting up his white tuft, I could see him studying the woman with great intensity, ready to make a protective move if any harm was to befall his family. ❖ I used scratchboard to capture his sharp features and the wispy white tuft of hair. ❖ Very soon, it was all over as the langur troops moved on to foraging another shrine, and the temple monkeys finally took over.

A short walk away is the shrine of Annapurna, Shiva's consort in her role as the provider of food aplenty. Her image sits majestically on a throne; in one hand is a ladle with which she generously doles out food contained in a vessel she holds with her other hand. She doesn't sit far from another well-known temple dedicated to Durga, a more fearsome form of the Hindu goddess. It is perched on a hillock, and I had to pass several troops of bold monkeys to get to the sanctum. The goddess is seated upon her leonine mount, her hands holding symbolic insignia, one of which grants eternal protection.

Later in the evening I hurried along the lanes into the Viswanatha shrine. Chants resonated from within the sanctum where priests, representing the Seven Sages of Hindu mythology, were performing worship.

Oblations innumerable were being offered in reverential worship to the sacred stone: milk, honey, flower garlands, and platefuls of sweets, fruits, and nuts. As camphor flames blazed high and incense filled the sanctum with wispy smoke, prayers rose to a crescendo.

No sooner did this worship conclude than pilgrims rushed in for a last glimpse of their divine protector before he retired to rest at midnight. But within hours he would be up again, awakened from cosmic slumber by priests in prayer. The Lord of Kasi never gets to rest; he needs to be ever vigilant so he can watch over the great city he rules and the people he protects within it. Not just the living but also the dead, who would continue to reside in the heavens forever. ❖

Paintings in the Making: Wanderings of a Young Artist

Pen on paper, 20 x 16, 16 x 20

As a twenty-one-year old, I found the ghats of Varanasi teeming with not just the living, but also the dead. ❖ The ones on their feet were mostly holy men (or ones that posed as them), older men and women, and tourists. ❖ While the older gentry didn't care to look up from their rituals to take notice of me, sadhus and some tourists would pause to watch what I was up to. I even made a few friends and promised to stay in touch, but thirty years ago snail mail was the only option, and I never really did. ❖ I must have made about sixty drawings during that time, just over a dozen consummated into displayable works of art. For the sake of authenticity, here are a few "art in the womb" pieces that are typically stashed away in my cabinet.

AHILYABHAI GHAT

VIEW OF DASASHWAMEDHA GHAT FROM RAJENDRA PRASAD GHAT

RAJA GHAT

A Riot of Color: Kedar Ghat

Acrylic on hardboard, 16 x 20

For two weeks, my family and I lodged in a decrepit ashram squished into one of the winding lanes above Kedar Ghat. As my parents busied themselves with preparations and consultations with priests for daily rituals, I would steal out with pen and paper, dashing through the dark lanes that cloaked the expanse of the eternal Ganges. I nudged the usual cows away and often had to push headlong into an onrush of pilgrims who were marching resolutely to the Kedareswar shrine. ❖ As the lane eventually trickled out into sunlight and spilled onto a vast vista, an assault of colors and a hush of quietude seemed to take over. ❖ Kedar Ghat is one of the most fascinating spots in this riot of habitation around the Ganges. To my right the funerary pyres of Hanuman Ghat blazed as a reminder of the inescapable mortality we all must face. Pilgrims smashed bubbly wet garments upon the stone steps in preparation for stretching them out in the sun. Pehlwans (muscled wrestlers) guffawed as they swished their mighty maces around, looking to see who was admiring their lissome physiques. Stray donkeys casually sauntered down the steps, foraging for offerings left behind. ❖ That morning the sun had just unleashed itself from the unrelenting rein of the clouds. A few boys were busy trying to get a kite in the sky. The inimitable stripes of Kedar Ghat gleamed in the sunlight. Even the murky waters near the banks, laden with flowery flotsam, were forced to reveal their reflections. ❖ I sketched this vigorously from a couple of angles, noting down the areas which seemed to dance in the light, capturing this in acrylic a couple of months later. ❖ Years later, despite exhibiting this with a "Not for Sale" sticker, I always have pleading—and flattering—inquiries to buy this piece of art. As one of the thwarted parties remarked, "It takes me right there!"

Jewels in the Forest: View from Temple IV

Whiteboard and ink, 9 x 12

"Whatever you do, don't back up," Roxy warned me as I stood gazing at the intricate roof comb of Temple IV before turning back to admire the landscape. The previous year a tourist posing for a picture, trying to get the forest as a backdrop, had stepped back a few precarious inches; that move proved fatal. ❖ I now stood on top of the Mesoamerican world. ❖ From this vantage point, I could see the fascinating swath of the Petén jungle all around me. Far in the distance were the twin temples of the royal couple. A bit to the right was the massive loom of Temple III, and far ahead of me yawned the hills that led to the ancient Maya kingdoms in Belize. ❖ I could imagine a time when traders would quarry precious jade from Quirigua, travel with their cargo in canoes down the river, then disembark at Tikal, carrying hundreds of pounds of prized stone upon their backs. There they would trade, then load their cargo on canoes and paddle into the Pacific Ocean towards the great Maya cities of Mexico. ❖ The dense canopy fascinated me the most. The roll of the verdant green, the sound of the hundreds of animals living in and off this lush vegetation, those stark tree trunks contrasting against the dark hues — all lent an air of mystery to the landscape. ❖ I needed to capture the spirit of the moment. I made a quick sketch and later used ink and whiteboard, scratching out the details.*

CHAPTER FIVE

GUATEMALA ❖ TIKAL

ON THE TRAIL OF THE JAGUAR

As a dry breeze swept through the landscape, I could hear the sounds of the jungle around me. Far in the distance towered the twin temples of the royal couple. To the right was the massive loom of Temple III, and poking out from the dense green canopy was the spire of Temple V.

In this vast, mathematically contrived setting, I easily transported myself to a time when shamans and astronomers would have stood upon the steps of their meticulously created stone universe, watching distant celestial bodies coursing in the heavens.

I was truly in the womb of an impenetrable jungle. Bloodcurdling growls of howler monkeys rent the air. Aztec parakeets heading back to their nests screeched above the canopy. A troop of spider monkeys performed their acrobatic feats high up in the trees. Ocellated turkeys in colorful raiment foraged the grounds, joined by a band of young coatis whose mother kept a watch for predators lurking in the thickets. Golden hues licked ancient stone monuments, singeing them orange and

The Morning Greeting

Watercolor, 14 x 11

I had just commenced my hike into the park, and though I was savvy to the sounds of the jungle — thanks to my experience in Costa Rica — I heard a loud rustle and started. A jaguar in pursuit? But I quickly realized that it was only the raucous howler monkeys leaving the park for their afternoon siestas. ❖ My sense of relief was abruptly shattered by hail of droppings from the skies. The culprit was a sluggish spider monkey high up in the trees that had just woken up and was performing his morning ablutions. As I glared at him, his expression was nonchalant and slightly puzzled, as if to ask, "OK, so what exactly did I do wrong?" ❖ I proceeded to recreate the monkey's expression with watercolor on cold-pressed paper. The dry-brush technique made the rendering of its furry tufts a lot easier.

pink as expectant minutes went by. It was 5:00 P.M. and the jungle orchestra had just commenced.

All this was an exotic setting for the ancient Maya ruins of Tikal, tucked away deep in the forests of El Petén in northeast Guatemala. I was among a handful of visitors witnessing this sunset spectacle from my perch on the Temple of Polaris in the North Acropolis.

More than a thousand years ago, this would have been the very scene of ancient

We descended the stone steps from the Temple of the Architect, hurrying for the sunset splendor at North Acropolis. ❖ "A pair of keel-billed toucans is spending a lot of time in that tree. See all the berries?" my guide, Roxy, said as we passed by the pyramid of Mundo Perdido. ❖ Sure enough, we could hear a sound similar to that of croaking frogs as we approached a clearing. ❖ It was a fairy tale moment — I was astounded by the beautiful colors. I was seeing toucans in the wild for the first time in my life! (My daughter, Amrita, claims to have spotted one among the zip-lines of Costa Rica, but I was very busy holding on for dear life at that point.) ❖ It was such a delight to see these beautiful birds up close. Their colors of yellow, green, blue, and red starkly contrasted against the green above and the dull gray stones of the structures. This pair was some twenty-five feet high in the trees, hopping from branch to branch and snacking on the delicious red berries punctuating the green canopy. One bird was restlessly hungry, while another paused and seemed to be studying us very demurely, almost posing for this picture. Its yellow breast against the dappled sunlight, the blotch of shocking red in its underbelly, and its orange beak glistening in the sun made for an unforgettable moment indeed. ❖ Only ink could capture nature's brilliance. I used a whiteboard, scratching out the details, and ink to add the colors.

Toucan Snacking
by Mundo Perdido

Whiteboard and ink, 12 x 9

Maya worship. The chief priest, adorned in headgear of brilliant quetzal feathers and a formidable necklace of jaguar claws, may have whispered mystic incantations that magically resounded across the sprawl of the Gran Plaza. The elite may have stood in reverence, fervently praying for rain to patter down upon their parched lands. For who better than the powerful shaman — through his compelling prayers and grasp of the secret lore of the stars — could commune with the gods in the heavens?

A Tall Majesty: View of Temple IV

Conté crayon, 11 x 14

"We saw a six-foot fer-de-lance (Lancehead Snake) this morning, right here," my guide Roxy exclaimed as we reached a clearing in the woods. "It was 4:00 A.M. and I was leading a sunrise tour," she added. "One man tried to shine his flashlight at it, and I told him to stop; it could have struck with deadly force!" ❖ It was now 4:00 P.M., but I looked around carefully for signs of remnant danger. Instead of frightening wildlife, I spotted a huge structure rising up above the jungle canopy. ❖ I had never before managed get a full view of Temple IV, the largest excavated structure in this complex. Even now, I could only see the steps leading to the top and its enormous roof comb. Somewhere up there were flecks of humanity — the tourists who had managed to climb its 265 feet to take in the panoramic stretch of the Maya kingdom lost in the unrelenting jungle canopy. ❖ Having perused my share of pictorial books on Maya culture, I could only imagine how this gargantuan structure, also known as the Temple of the Two-Headed Snake, must have looked back in its day. At the sight of its looming roof comb from afar, traders from other Maya kingdoms must have heaved a sigh of relief, having traversed dense forests and treacherous rivers before finally reaching their port of call. ❖ Of course, things had changed; in those days, the temple was clothed in its grandeur of stucco and paint and likely glistened with cadmium hues in the evening light. All the noises of a civilization would have resounded through a throbbing city, unobstructed by vine and shrubbery as it stood today. No one knows for certain if this monument was meant to be a tomb or a sacred shrine, an observatory or simply a vantage marker of those times. ❖ I used a thicker sepia pencil for capturing the elemental essence of ancient stone towering above the landscape, precisely as I viewed it from among the humble thickets where I stood.

I had been plotting a trip to Tikal since I was eighteen, but in the same way the dreadful minefields of Cambodia had prevented me from taking a trip to Angkor until recently, the fear of highway robbers armed with machetes and automatics kept me from visiting Guatemala. Now, more than thirty years later and emboldened by the crowds of the "2012 apocalypse" jamboree, I ventured into this jewel of the jungles.

It was a hot and clammy morning as I set out on my sixty-five-minute ride from

my hotel in the town of Santa Elena towards the Tikal complex. Just as in most of Central America, and particularly in Guatemala, the b'aktun ceremonies heralding the much-feared "2012 End of the World" had recently concluded here with song, dance, and prayer.

My guide at Tikal was a scholarly woman named Roxy Ortiz. My ignorance of the desperately needed Spanish in these parts was easily overshadowed by her fluency in English and profound knowledge of the Maya legends she had amassed over her thirty-three years as a tour guide.

The Moonlight Supper

Pastel on board, 10 x 12

The wildlife in Tikal fascinated me. Everywhere there were coatis, parakeets, ocellated turkeys, howler and spider monkeys, dreadfully poisonous snakes, and even the rare ocelot or jaguar. ❖ "How many jaguars have you seen here lately?" I asked Roxy. ❖ "Several!" she replied, adding that the best way out of one of these encounters was to simply keep your distance and look unperturbed. ❖ Tikal by moonlight is bewitchingly captivating. As a full moon rose up above Temple II, its silvery beams lit up the tomb of Lord Chocolate. I would love to have spent a night by the ruins if not for the pesky park employees who walk around at night making sure everything is in order. ❖ And for good reason. Apparently, a year ago a couple of errant tourists decided to overnight in the ruins and climbed up one of the pyramids in the Gran Plaza. Their presence went unnoticed until the moon was in full shine at 1:00 A.M. A jaguar was on the prowl in the area and the now-awakened tourists cowered, screaming for help as the curious animal decided to investigate the human scent. Roxy said the miscreants were only too glad to be apprehended by the park authorities! ❖ Suddenly my ears perked up to the sound of scurrying feet, and I noticed this young band of coatis out for supper. The silvery fur of one fulsome animal against the pale moonbeams and the backdrop of the huge stone monument was an inviting setting for a pastel drawing.

AN ANCIENT SETTLEMENT

Tikal's earliest settlements started in the fifth century B.C.E., peaking to glory during the Classic Period, about 200 - 900 C.E. Then it suddenly was stifled by vine and tree. Rediscovered in 1848, its lineage has been lost in mystery, just like its colorful pyramids and glittering streets, vast riches and treasures.

Historians speak of an ancient connection with distant Teotihuacan in Mexico, while legend traces the history of Tikal to the powerful kingdom of Mirador, which was flourishing at a time when Tikal was but a dense forest. Later, in the fifth century, a strong nexus formed among the powerful states of Dos Pilos, Caracol, and Calakmul, which resulted in a humiliating defeat for Tikal. Later rulers revolted, prominently Jasaw Chan K'awiil, also known as Ah Cacao or Lord Chocolate, who eventually freed his kingdom from the shackles of enemy rule.

"At five feet ten inches tall, Lord Chocolate must have been a force to reckon with," Roxy remarked as we walked along his 154-foot-high funerary pyramid known as Temple I or the Temple of the Great Jaguar (pages 92-3). Unlike many Maya pyramids in other parts of Central America, these structures were characterized by limestone roof combs carved with beautiful glyphs and figurines that rose up from above the top of these pyramids.

"You're seeing only the skeletons of a civilization," Roxy said as we passed by these monumental structures. "Imagine those years when these would have been covered with thick stucco painted in the bold Maya colors of yellow, red, blue, and white. Imagine instead," she added, "a magically wonderful city!"

Just facing the Temple of the Great Jaguar, a shorter Temple II, the Temple of Masks (pages 86-7), was built in honor of Lord Chocolate's wife, Lady Twelve Macaw, to commemorate their love.

Pedro, King of the Swamp

Colored pencil, 12 x 9

My wife, Ramaa, named him Pedro, as if in response to the bumblebee my children named Roberto, and the coati they called Ernesto. In this trip to Guatemala, everything seemed to have a Spanish flair. ❖ It was a lazier morning that found us nursing the aches and bug bites of the Tikal jungle from the day before. We were having breakfast in our hotel in Santa Elena, which skirted Lake Petén Itzá, facing the strip of land that connects this town to ancient Flores. ❖ I had seen turtles, ducks, and statuesque cormorants in these waters but never this colorful creature that suddenly appeared, as if by whim, upon a wooden post. ❖ He was motionless as we first took notice of him, but when he started vigorously bobbing his head up and down, my family had fun posing questions such as "Are you Pedro?" and "Do you have children?" to which the response seemed to be an eternal affirmative. ❖ The colors of this iguana were fascinating in the morning sunlight. I could see bright red, yellow, green, blue, as well as a glistening orange on his dewlap and the sheen of the scales on his back. ❖ I made a quick sketch, took a snap and later recreated Pedro in colored pencil far away in my Chicago studio.

On the day of the equinox, one temple's shadow would embrace the other; as that day turned to evening the other would reciprocate. In this way, the beloveds were united forever even after their deaths. Legend has it that Lady Twelve Macaw's father refused to part with his daughter's hand to a mere vassal, at which point the determined suitor vowed to overthrow the enemy king of Calakmul and also build a pyramid within ten years. He completed both projects in eight!

Drama upon Stone:
Sunset behind Temple II,
Viewed from the North Acropolis

Acrylic on canvas board, 11 x 14

In this expanse of a spectacular jungle, I was but a small brushstroke in nature's endless canvas. ❖ It was 5:30 P.M. on a beautiful December evening, probably the pleasantest time in these parts. High up on the steps of the North Acropolis, I stood awestruck by the panorama of the twin monuments of the Gran Plaza painted by the setting sun. Temple I, the monument of Jasaw Chan K'awiil, was struck aflame with an orange glow. The sun was sinking into the trees behind the pyramid of his beloved Lady Twelve Macaw. ❖ Keeping up the cadence, the treetops too picked up the ruddy glow, offering a breathtaking backdrop to these ancient structures scattered all across the jungle. The verdant grounds were punctuated by flecks of colors, silent stelae and forgotten columns enlivened by a parade of ocellated turkeys, coatis, and a handful of people hurrying to find a vantage point in the courtyard to witness the unveiling of a divine painting. ❖ At that very moment a couple of coatis sprang upon the stone steps for a last snack of berries before they retired up into the trees, high and far from the reach of lusty jaguars that would start their prowl very soon. ❖ As I quickly sketched the vista before me, I knew I couldn't compete with that Greater Artist with a more magical canvas who wielded her brush with consummate skill. I attempted drawing this in ink and watercolor, but in vain; these mediums seemed impotent in capturing the brilliance of the scene. I eventually broke out the panorama into two scenes and used acrylic, in a humble bid to replicate the spirit of that moment.

Peeping through the Rock: A Temple IV Vista

Watercolor, 11 x 14

"Look! From this side!" an excited tourist shouted in uncontained surprise. ❖ I was standing upon the highest step in the North Acropolis, watching the sweep of the Gran Plaza and waiting for the sun to sink, when I saw this man running excitedly with his camera towards an opening to my right. ❖ Had I been the first one to make this discovery, I would probably have reacted the same way. Framed by solid sandstone blocks was a narrow opening through which I could see the distant spire of Temple IV. A carpet of green canopy separated me from this majesty looming in the distance. It seemed remarkable to me that we had come so far. Just an hour ago I had been admiring the jungle vista standing upon a ledge on Temple IV. ❖ From a distance, I could see several open slits atop its roof comb from where astronomers of yesteryear would have tracked the path of Venus. ❖ "Look up there!" Roxy suddenly exclaimed as a flock of leviathans winged above in the skies. Squinting in the sun, we couldn't make out what these were, but Roxy guessed these were large waterbirds driven out by a storm brewing in the Pacific. ❖ There was something captivating about this view that I needed to preserve forever. I used a Chinese bamboo brush with watercolor, using several layers of washes to recreate the colors of that evening.

MARVELS OF ARCHITECTURE

The grounds of Gran Plaza forms a vast ceremonial site flanked by the North Acropolis and this majestic pair of pyramids. As we walked south, we came upon a cluster of buildings, part of the Central Acropolis. This section once brimmed with magnificent palaces, large reservoirs, and wide streets. Passing a huge courtyard that separated the commoners' quarters from those of the elite, we walked through what must have once been beautiful buildings with corbelled arches and painted stucco friezes.

The engineers for this project had truly mastered the art of constructing multistoried mansions. I had to remind myself all along that in creating these masterpieces there

was no wheel or beast of burden deployed, nor metal used. The Maya carved and chiseled their civilization using only flint and obsidian.

I quickly climbed the steps of the Five-Tiered Palace to take in the view of the tree-lined skyline dotted with spires of stone.

"Only nine percent of Tikal has been excavated so far," Roxy told me as I looked from the terrace at the grassy mound that was once the South Acropolis. At the height of its glory in the ninth century, Tikal may have sprawled across an eighty-one square mile area, a grand city of some 120,000 commoners and five hundred noblemen.

The ancient Maya were marvelous architects who had the gumption to build a city where there was no nearby body of water. Digging up limestone blocks from the ground to build their ceremonial structures, they plastered these depressions, transforming them into gigantic water tanks. They had then proceeded to construct an extensive system of dikes and channels to collect every precious drop of rainwater that would then be fed to these reservoirs.

Much like engineering, astronomy and the solar calendar were an integral part of Maya life. Not all pyramids were built to be only tombs — like the Egyptians, the Maya built some specifically to track the course of the celestial bodies in the skies. Agriculture was the lifeblood of Maya society, so marking seasons and perfecting the solar calendar were elemental in ensuring their survival and prosperity.

High upon such a pyramid, the head priest would stand with a plumb bob tracking the sun's position, instructing the workers on the ground to mark that spot each day of the year. The process needed to be so precise that notches have been inscribed upon the top of such pyramids where their feet would need to be aligned for taking a measurement. Such a project would take several years to perfect, accounting for solstice adjustments or days of heavy rain when the sun wouldn't simply be visible for months.

The position of Venus — or Chak Ek' — in the skies was equally important, as the Maya believed that this mystical companion of the sun deeply influenced their lives with portentous forebodings. Major "star wars" would be launched when the planet was at its brightest, accompanied by bloody conquests and sacrifice.

"There are over six major pyramids that have been excavated so far in Tikal," Roxy said as we came across these gigantic buildings in the park. Some like Temple I were funerary monuments, while some like Temples III, IV or V may have also served as astronomical observatories and ceremonial spots for connecting with the gods in heaven.

There were also several twin pyramid complexes scattered throughout the park. Every k'atun — twenty years — the extant king, beseeching the gods for continued prosperity, undertook the mammoth task of building a pair of pyramids. The completion was marked by ritual bloodletting and sacrifices followed by prayer and dancing.

Older than most other structures here, the Grand Pyramid of the Lost World was also the astronomical observatory. In this extensive complex also known as Mundo Perdido, there were several ballgame courts. From the bleachers, the chosen young, groomed for the game of pok-ta-pok, would watch players from both teams use all parts of their body except their hands and feet to guide a leather ball through a hoop mounted high on a stone wall. After the elimination rounds, the main game would be played in the massive court of the Gran Plaza, witnessed by hundreds of people. The penalty for the losing side would mean death by sacrifice.

High above the tree line at 212 feet, Temple IV, the Temple of the Two-Headed Snake (pages 76, 81, and 89) is the second tallest structure in all of Mesoamerica, next only to La Danta in nearby Mirador. One of the few structures here that I was permitted to climb, the ascent took me ten nimble minutes upon wooden planks, bringing me to the top of this world. As a dry breeze swept through the landscape, I could see the expansive canopy of the Petén jungle all around me, speckled by distant structures from ancient times. Far beyond the blue hills stretched Belize and its own bygone kingdoms of the Maya.

Later in the evening, in preparation for the spectacle of sunset, I climbed up the steps of the North Acropolis, then looked down upon the majestic swath of the Gran Plaza. To my left was the resting place of Lord Chocolate, facing Lady Twelve Macaw's monument. Ahead of me loomed Temple V, the second tallest structure here, and to the right was the Lost World. Through a hole in the stone to my far right Temple IV stood tall.

Where vines and shrub now ravaged, a thousand years ago here would have stretched a vast city with magnificent buildings and wide streets. Chants of shamans and the shouts of civilization would have resonated where silence today is broken only by the sounds of the jungle.

Although several theories are posited, no one knows for certain how such a great civilization vanished altogether. Did the infamous one-hundred-year drought dry up the fields and reservoirs, taking a fatal toll on the populace? Did cholera ravage the population, destroying the lakes and the civilizations that lived around it? Did the construction of those monumental buildings prove too costly, snuffing out the prosperity of the Maya?

Only those lurking jaguars might know. The jungle has a way of keeping its secrets. ❖

A Curious Visitor: Sunset on the Temple of the Great Jaguar

Acrylic on canvas board, 11 x 14

After the toucan encounter near Mundo Perdido, Roxy took us to the North Acropolis. There was only a handful of tourists that evening, but the seating spots upon the top of the steps were all taken. ❖ *The ocellated turkeys in Tikal were extremely shy birds; they strutted around unabashedly in the Gran Plaza but scampered away when approached. As I looked at the splendid vista ahead of me, I was transfixed by the changing orange glow upon Temple I. The golden orb was sinking below the trees, behind Temple II, even as breathless moments went by. All of a sudden a shy turkey, which I had earlier observed hopping around the stelae, now pounced upon a ledge. It stood motionless, as if it too was transfixed by the grandeur of the moment.* ❖ *I quickly sketched the scene using splashes of watercolor to capture those splendorous hues. Later, in my studio I ended up painting this in acrylic to duplicate the brilliance of the scene.*

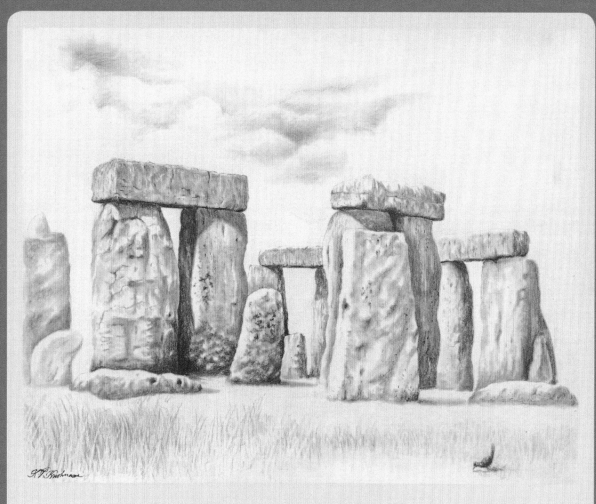

The Hungry Blackbird

Pencil on paper, 11 x 14

Right before me was a busy blackbird pecking away at the grass. Behind this carefree creature stood the circle of somber sandstone spectators. Four thousand years ago, this procession of megaliths may have looked a lot more complete, their surfaces less weatherworn. ❖ Pencil on a heavy Bristol paper was the best way to capture the smoothness of the stones, their speckles and undulations. I spent a full half hour under the sun — no shade as far as the eye could see — capturing the parade of these stone giants. Later, in the comfort of my Chicago studio, I used a blending stump and some soft pencils to good effect, capturing the light and shade of the late-afternoon scene. ❖ Of course, the restless blackbird took off in a few seconds, only to be replaced a few minutes later by sheep and ravens.

CHAPTER SIX

UNITED KINGDOM ❖ STONEHENGE

SECRET OF THE STONE SENTINELS

Awestruck, I was walking the grounds of an age-old enigma that bore no signature of an artist nor a suggestive nick of the artisan's chisel. No one knows what race crafted such a stupendous structure or how they dragged gigantic boulders from faraway mountains, shaping them to perfection, then arranging these megaliths in an esoteric circle for a purpose unknown.

Here, an ancient people erected a temple of stones to worship the sacred solstice, that surreal moment when the first feeble rays of the sun pierce through a pair of massive Heel Stones, smiling down upon the cold altar of the innermost circle. This evoked an exhilaration of fulfillment among the fervent masses assembled. This is what they had traveled from distant lands to see.

I stood gazing at wildflowers speckled in the roll of the verdant lea. Puffy white clouds sailed in the blue summer sky. A murder of raucous ravens and the distant fleck of sheep completed a typical English pastoral scene here in the rolling plains of Wiltshire.

Judging by the crowds, however, this was surely the site of a spectacle and not just an idyllic setting. In this landscape were also huddled several gigantic sandstone

A Girl in Tears: Raven upon a Sarsen

Scratchboard, 9 x 12

Sheep and ravens pretty much made up the fauna of the green Wiltshire flats. While the former were quietly grazing a good distance away, the ravens were making themselves heard from atop the gigantic stone sentries. ❖ I watched one bold bird hopping about from sarsen to lintel. Fancifully, I named him "Carbon," and I could pick him out from wherever I stood by his sheer bulk. He seemed to be not just foraging for food but also picking up glittering objects from the grass, then taking off to some unknown destination. At one point, things got exciting when a little girl screamed out crying as the bird targeted a chunk of cookie that had fallen from her hand onto the grass. A deft swoop was followed by a peck and a quick toss of the beak for a better grip before he flew up to a sarsen to proclaim his conquest for all to hear. ❖ It was an eye-catching moment as he cawed from his perch with the bulge of the tenon contrasting against the pale skies. ❖ His gossamer feathers glistened against the afternoon sun. I took a few photographs and chose a scratchboard that would enable me to capture the glossy feathers and the harsh texture of ancient stone.

sentinels arranged in a circle, standing as they have for centuries. Four thousand years ago, the scene here could have been virtually the same, except that instead of ancient Britons heaving enormous slabs of stone, today camera-toting tourists mill around, taking in their sight of a lifetime from all photographic angles.

I was in enigmatic Stonehenge whose history will be forever shrouded in eternal mystery. Wild theories abound as to its origins, but no one really knows when or why such a gargantuan effort was undertaken. Over centuries, stories have been handed down of sun worship, sacrifice cults, healing stones, Druid rituals, astronomical calendars, Atlanteans, and even extraterrestrial powers that may have caused such a unique monument to be built in such an unremarkable part of England. Of this place, New Age cultists talk of ley lines: mysterious energy vortexes that crisscross this region, exuding the raw power of nature.

One sunny June morning I signed up for a bus tour that left from the bustle of Victoria Station in central London. Zooming along speedy expressways, we reached the parking lot of Stonehenge in just a couple of hours. What a contrast: on one side of a busy A303 road, lumbering trucks and noisy cars whizzed by, while on the other was a silent circle of megaliths standing in a vast plain just as they have for thousands of years.

Walking closer, I could feel a becalming quiet as I stared at these timeless boulders shaped by human hands. Thousands of years ago, sacred chants may have resonated from within a timber hut surrounded by the stone circle, marking another summer solstice. Pilgrims may have turned ecstatic as the first sliver of sunlight streaked between two gigantic Heel Stones, touching down upon the altar. Each year, they came here in droves to witness this celestial event, mooring their boats by the banks of the Avon.

A MONUMENTAL PROJECT

As our group skirted the protective rope around the monument, Andrew, our guide, explained how Stonehenge was likely created in three stages over a span

Raucous Shrieks: The Vast Vista

Acrylic on paper, 16 x 20

As I stood in the quiet sweep of the Wiltshire plains, it seemed unbelievable that this very spot had been the bustling site of human activity four thousand years ago. What had driven an ancient Neolithic race to construct such an esoteric edifice upon this site? ❖ Raw muscle dug out a circular ditch 320 feet wide, then built an embankment using stone, bones, and antlers. A timber structure was later built in the center, presumably used for worship or healing. Over sixty sacred bluestones were hauled from faraway Preseli Mountains in Wales to be placed in a circular arrangement. Andrew, my guide, readily confessed that no one really knows how these four-ton blocks could have been moved from such a remote terrain, or whether they were hauled on land or sailed in on boats. ❖ A series of large sandstone slabs were then arranged in an outer formation that became known as the Sarsen Circle. Each of the thirty sarsens, lugged from Marlborough Downs about twenty miles away, stood nearly twenty feet tall and weighed close to thirty tons. Amazingly, these were linked by ten-foot-long lintels forming a perfect circle of stones. ❖ As I watched this spectacle, a few sheep, common in this part of the world, strayed into the foreground. Noisy ravens flapped above, looking for a lucky morsel. The rolling green, dotted with visitors and wildflowers, contrasted against the backdrop of stunning blue skies and puffy white clouds. ❖ I sketched the scene with watercolor pencils on my pad, later recreating this picture in my Chicago studio.

Lost My Partner: Lone Heel Stone

Watercolor, 9 x 12

On the way to the parking lot, some distance from the main scene of action, I noticed this lone sarsen stone, sixteen feet high. My guide had explained that this was one of a pair, but the other was missing. Several centuries ago these two sentinels towered outside the stone circle, greeting the last rays of the setting sun. ❖ As I did a quick watercolor sketch of this oddly shaped colossus, I imagined how pilgrims may have trudged up from the River Avon to witness the play of the solstice — a divine drama in which these stones were key members of the cast. ❖ To create this painting, especially the spotty texture of the stone, I stippled drops of paint upon uneven gobs of water generously applied to paper.

of some fifteen hundred years. Around 3100 B.C.E., an ancient people dug out a wide circular ditch and constructed an embankment using stone, bones, and antlers. All this with sheer muscle and resolve.

Centuries later, a wooden structure was built in the center for worship or healing. Starting in 2400 B.C.E., and lasting until the site's abandonment in 1600 B.C., a glorious transformation took place of which there is no record. A mystical parade of gigantic stones was erected within and around the hallowed ditch, metamorphosing what was once just a simple timber temple into a majestic and awe-inspiring structure.

Interestingly, henges, Neolithic earthwork comprising an upraised mound that encloses an inner ditch, aren't an uncommon sight in this part of the world. Earlier, I visited a large stone circle in Avebury, twenty-six miles away, and to my surprise, I learned there are more than nine hundred such circles throughout the British Isles!

As I walked around the rope circle at Stonehenge, I saw several types of stones that made up the monument. Many were fallen, missing or broken, having weathered a relentless assault by the elements, builders, and overzealous pilgrims alike through the ages. The circular arrangement was thus broken and I could only imagine how the monument must have looked in its years of glory.

Andrew explained that the innermost horseshoe arrangement was made up of sacred bluestones hauled from distant mountains in Wales. A series of outer sandstone megaliths, known as the Sarsen Circle, was later erected in a circular formation. What is most astonishing is that each slab looms twenty feet tall, and these blocks are joined together at the top by huge lintels carved into an arc, which when all joined make a perfect circle. Another horseshoe arrangement of stones known as trilithons was created between the bluestones and the outer circle.

Farther away stood a solitary Heel Stone sticking up from the ground and facing the blue sky (left). A few thousand years ago it would have had a companion stone that together greeted the first sunrays of the solstice dawn.

How these mighty stones were hoisted, propped into the ground, carved to perfection, and joined together — before the discovery of iron or bronze — is the essence of the mystery at Stonehenge!

Closer to the Stones

Watercolor, 12 x 16

My guide Andrew explained that Stonehenge was created in three stages over fifteen hundred years, starting around 3100 B.C. Alas, all the hustle and bustle vanished as mysteriously as it had started; the site was pretty much deserted by 1100 B.C., predating the Druids and before the first Romans arrived in Britain. ❖ I walked closer to these huge sarsens. Closer to the stones I noticed the moss that coats the gray boulders in green patches. I could see undulations upon stone, much like delicate folds of drapery. Ancient man must have patiently chipped away at these blocks using blunt antlers and animal bone. ❖ I painted a quick watercolor sketch on the spot, lest I was unable to create this vista of colors from sheer memory. That evening, I recreated this vividly-impressed scene in the privacy of my London hotel suite.

An Enigma Eternal

Two thousand years of frenetic activity must surely have had some purpose, and scientists and archaeologists have tried hard to determine the purpose with the use of high-powered gadgets. To no avail, unfortunately. Furthermore, numerous legends have only added to the aura of mystery that surrounds Stonehenge. Irish folklore maintains that giants carried these stones all the way from Africa. According to a later story, Merlin the magician, upon orders from the king to build a memorial, used his spells to lift the stones from Ireland.

Was this site, considered one of the most powerful centers of energy on earth, meant for a congregation of the holiest? Its popularity as a healing center was so prominent that for several centuries, droves of visitors washed the stones with water and then bathed themselves with it to treat their maladies.

Strange discoveries have added to the confusion. Why was an Anglo-Saxon nobleman ritually executed on this spot by a hail of flint-tipped arrows shot from short range? Why was a Roman skeleton discovered here in a ditch, even though we know that Romans

set foot in Britain only in 43 C.E., long after Stonehenge had lost its secret purpose?

As I stood under the long shadows of the stones on that summer evening, ubiquitous ravens hopped atop the lintels. Below them, tourists milled endlessly around the perimeter.

What sights have these vigilant stones watched over the ages? How many laborers toiled over the years and how did they haul these mammoth slabs from mountains miles away? What secret rituals took place within its sanctum?

Much like the Rosetta Stone that changed the way we look at Egypt today, archaeologists may one day discover the missing key that will reveal the best-kept secrets of the Stonehenge people: secrets handed down for fifteen centuries before they came to be suddenly buried, completely forgotten. ❖

6 P.M.: Sunset through the Stones

Watercolor, 11 x 14

Most of the other tourists had boarded their immense buses and were long gone. ❖ In a splendid display of colors, Stonehenge was dressing itself for yet another rapturous moment. The sun quickly sank below the horizon, splashing the skies in gray, orange, yellow, and mauve. I didn't have the luxury of visiting during the solstice, but I positioned myself at a spot where I could see the sun make its journey across the skies. ❖ I noticed that it was getting cooler. Vapory exhalations of mist rose from the ground, adding to the powerful sense of enigma that soaked the place. A sunbeam slanted down, cleaving a sarsen, smiting the haze below. At 6 P.M., the sun sank down, framed by a lintel and a pair of megaliths, its rays aimed straight at me. The stones glistened, their pockmarks lit up by hues of gold. A lone fellow tourist walked around the circle, clearly lost in this amazing moment. ❖ As I applied eight washes in hurried succession, I humbly realized the futility of trying to record a divine drama upon a two-dimensional strip of paper.

Eating My Coffee: Evening at Wadi Rum

Pastel on paper, 11 x 14

The bumpy jeep strained along the dunes. Far away, nearly lost in a cloud of raging sands, I could make out the silhouette of a camel caravan trundling its way into the horizon. ❖ *The village of Wadi Rum is only a two-hour drive heading north from Aqaba. Bedouin-led treks on camels, as well as the more modern jeep tours, start from this coastal town — the only human habitation for miles around. Camels have to "tank up" at water troughs before embarking on their long journeys into the desert.* ❖ *I wasn't too keen on riding a camel after a painful experience just a couple of days before. The hurrying wind beat into my face as I clambered into an open jeep instead. Along the way I could see a number of nomadic Bedouin families, inhabitants of Wadi Rum.* ❖ *We stopped along the way, and I found myself under a tent sipping Arabian coffee, which I found distastefully viscous. Still, I pretended to love every slurp of it lest I offend my Bedouin host.* ❖ *Our entourage then sped towards the Seven Pillars of Wisdom, a geological formation immortalized by Lawrence of Arabia. Somewhere on the way back, I paused to watch an amazing sunset. A herd of goats was on the loose, scouring the scrub in search of the rare green nibble. A shepherd in his tunic, holding his crook, stood upon a rocky promontory. Behind him was a cinematic backdrop of red rocks painted golden in the palette of colors that was the sky.* ❖ *I clicked a few photos. I recreated this scene on cold-pressed paper to capture the texture of the cliffs, using a blending stump to smooth the rocks.*

CHAPTER SEVEN

JORDAN ❖ PETRA

TREASURES IN THE RED DESERT

Had I chanced upon a moment from the Arabian Nights?

I lingered among stone genies that could cast a spell, among ancient gods and goddesses who might be waiting to grant my most impossible wishes.

The landscape around me was like a storybook setting: rose-red rocks carved into fantastic shapes by hurrying winds and sands, riddled with multistoried dwellings where people once lived with the dead. The history of this necropolis goes back many centuries, when ancient wayfarers and their caravans crisscrossed the desert, laden with spices, silks, and treasures bound for exotic lands.

A cool wind scattered the sands in a hazy frenzy. An unending expanse of carved rocks sprawled in this part of the Jordanian desert. Hundreds of tombs sprinkled in the silent mountains reminded me of a long-ago past when mysterious peoples vanished as fleetingly as the camel caravans that have traversed these dunes over the centuries.

My family and I traveled here to beautiful Petra, the secret city of the Nabataeans, a nomadic tribe from ancient Arabia. We took a group tour from Tel Aviv, and our bus crossed the border from the Israeli city of Eilat, reaching the legendary Jordanian port of Aqaba. As we sped along the highway, Bashar, our guide, talked to us about the desert and the lost city of Petra nestled in those imposing rocks.

The ruddy village of Wadi Rum was only a two-hour drive from the blue waters of the Red Sea lapping Aqaba. Of Lawrence of Arabia fame, Wadi Rum is a silent landscape of ancient riverbeds and pastel-colored stretches of desert interspersed with tall sandstone mountains. This lonely expanse looked to me like the surface of the moon, with crags and craters taking on subtly different hues throughout the day and night.

A two-hour drive from Wadi Rum brought us to the great city of Petra, a sight too breathtaking to take in one measure. Once known as the "Rose-Red City," this secret of the Nabataeans was well-preserved through the ages by the Bedouins who believed that untold treasures lay interred within those monuments. This was truly a natural fortress carved out of craggy rocks, unknown to Western civilization for centuries.

Ancient Petra was first occupied around 600 B.C.E. by the Nabataeans. A buzzing hub of rich caravan routes that crisscrossed the sands over history, the place reached its glory under Roman rule in the second century C.E. As ships slowly displaced the long treks over sand, the place fell into disuse and was lost to the world for over a thousand years.

It was only later in the early nineteenth century that Johann Burckhardt, an adventurous Swiss explorer, rediscovered the city. This dauntless man converted to Islam, mastered Arabic, and befriended the suspicious Bedouins, risking his life in the bargain.

MYSTERIOUS MECHANICS

Who were the Nabataeans?" our guide, Bashar, asked.

I quickly realized he was tossing out a trick question. As it turns out, no

Genies Galore: Djinn Blocks

Conté crayon, 12 x 16

What spirits were those strange structures hiding? Did they entrap genies? Were they now standing as staunch sentinels to ward off evil from these lands? ❖ To get to the gorge that would open out to a wonder of wonders, we had to traverse the valley of Bab as-Siq from the village of Wadi Musa. We came upon these odd structures scattered throughout the park. Bashar told the group that these were in fact the earliest tombs found in Petra. They could have been carved in the form of Dushara, an ancient pre-Islamic god of the Nabataeans, who was often represented as a block of stone. ❖ It was a bright morning. I had broken away from the group and was idly watching horse and donkey "taxis" ferrying tourists. Then my eye was caught by the slanting sun vibrantly lighting up the red rocks in warm hues. ❖ To capture the essence of the ruddy rocks that sprawled all around me, I did several drawings using Conté crayons on textured paper.

Fruitless Factoids: The Obelisk Tomb and the Bab as-Siq Triclinium

Conté crayon, 11 x 14

Walking further along the Bab as-Siq pathway, not far from the djinn blocks, I chanced upon this wonderful vista. I had strayed far away from my tour group and even risked climbing up a rocky perch to get a better perspective. The sun was cleaving through the Obelisk Tomb, which featured four pyramidal spires rising up from the rocks. To an ancient race these blocks were an embodiment of their sacred gods — divinities without shape or attribute. ❖ Did these four tombs belong to a Nabataean family of those times? Could this structure have an Egyptian influence? ❖ Alas, no one seemed to know. Opposite the tomb, about fifteen feet atop another red rock not far from where I perched, I noticed an inscription in Greek and what was probably Nabataean script, making this beautiful spot all the more mysterious as a confluence of cultures. As I stood here lost to the world, a visibly irritated Bashar, worried about the group's timetable, caught up with me. He took a moment to explain that the inscription indicates that the tomb belongs to one 'Abdmank, son of 'Akayus, son of Shullay, son of 'Utaih, and his progeny for eternity and beyond — and yes, I felt much better knowing this! ❖ The triclinium located below the Obelisk Tomb is a Nabataean-style dining chamber that probably served as a ritual gathering place before the actual burial took place. ❖ A sepia-tone Conté crayon sketch captured this scene. I used an electric eraser to capture the effect of sunlight pouring in from between the rocks.

one really knows the answer. There was a popular theory that the Nabataeans were an Arabic race who were master hydraulic engineers of the desert. They channeled water from inaccessible springs through terracotta pipes virtually hidden from human eyes, tapping it all the way through to their city.

The Nabataeans were also builders of great skill, carving their intricate city from obdurate rock. Working from the top down, they sliced off huge slabs of stone, using the ledge thus formed as scaffolding for masons to stand upon. Great pillars and massive walls were carved before another slab was removed in the same way, creating another platform from which other facades and columns were crafted and deep chambers hollowed out. In this way, the master builders were able to descend ten stories to the valley floor below.

The city was divided into the necropolis, which houses thousands of tombs in secret burial places, and the more distant cardo and marketplace beyond, where lay old monasteries, houses, and palaces of royal kinsmen. Nearby sites hidden by valleys and red massifs continued this fascinating story backwards in time to centuries before these Nabataean wonders ever came to be.

Snaking through the Siq

Approaching Petra through the necropolis, I saw strange-looking obelisks on both sides that served as burial places. Many of them were family tombs — some three stories high — marking the mortuary of a wealthy Nabataean household. I walked past inscriptions and came upon large stone cubes with seemingly no purpose.

"These are the djinn blocks," Bashar noted. Probably constructed as talismans for warding off the malevolent unknown, over twenty-six such structures are found along this colonnaded pathway (page 109).

I then visited what must have been a vast dam. Built around the first century B.C.E., these consummate architects wanted to contain the

Cliffs on Fire!: Walking into the Gorge

Watercolor, 14 x 11

We had been tramping for well over two miles from where our tour bus was parked. The valley of Bab as-Siq had narrowed into a slit-like gorge where three-hundred-foot cliffs stared down upon us puny flecks of tourists. At times, we found ourselves straining through sieve-like openings as tight as a mere ten feet wide. ❖ A cool breeze wafting from behind kept us company. The path was a downward slope, and I knew that I would have to use all my energies to paint and draw what I could at this point, since the climb up would surely wear me out. ❖ We rounded a bend, and I came upon this sight. The sun was tearing through an opening, setting fire to ancient cliffs painted with a splash of colors. I could see red, blue, purple, green, and ocher on the mineral-laden walls, witness to the trudge of humans for over two thousand years. Everywhere I looked there were inscriptions and shrines that would have been evident to pilgrims and weary merchants as they hurried on their way to the city center and its marketplace. It was simply spectacular. ❖ Marching along behind the other tourists was my wife, wearing a white straw hat and holding the hand of our five-year-old. She was looking admiringly at the cliffs that rose on either side. The red stones were set aflame by the magic of the slanting sunlight. ❖ I sketched this scene on my notepad, carefully noting the colors I observed. I later recreated it in my Tel Aviv apartment over several graduated washes.

floodwaters of Wadi Musa, preventing them from rushing down through the gorge in a post-winter torrent. Bashar explained that flash floods as recently as a couple of decades ago proved fatal for tourists, since there was no way past the trap of cruel rocks that loomed on either side.

Surely we were approaching that narrow, deep gorge, the Siq, whose cleft winds whipped for over half a mile past a massive wall of rock (left; page 114). At some points, the Siq squeezes to a rift less than twelve feet wide, and its vertical walls tower to a height of three hundred feet, making Petra one of the best-defended cities of all time. "The Nabataeans worshipped the deity Dushara," Bashar told us. Dushara seemed to be a cultist symbol, often depicted with his consort Al-'Uzza. I could see traces of visitors who had come from lands as far away as Syria, some carving out in the rock a supplicatory image of the god Dushara in human form.

A cool breeze tore through the narrow canyon, chilling me in my steps. In half an hour, I reached the end of the Siq. Through the cleft of the canyon was one of the most impressive sights I'd ever seen in all my years of travel. Here I experienced a thrill that was as dramatic to me then as it must have been to a lone camel-rider centuries ago. Turning the corner and passing beneath two overhanging cliffs, I abruptly stepped back in awe at the sight of Al Khazneh, the Treasury, the royal tomb styled after a Greek temple (page 117). This is Petra's most famous monument.

This graceful structure, standing about 130 feet tall, was carved out of solid rock into the side of a mountain. It stood quiet in a secret clearing, hugged by red massifs on either side; it look just as it must have when it was first carved two thousand years ago. The Bedouins always wanted to believe that there were untold treasures buried in a large stone urn above. Many vandals had tried their luck, as I could see by the numerous bullet holes that riddled the facade. However, Al Khazneh was just another tomb, though perhaps for a very notable personage of the time.

Beyond a stairway cut in the rock and along the Street of Facades were hundreds of temples, royal tombs, houses, banquet halls, marketplaces, and paved streets. I eyed what looked like a gigantic Roman theater in one of the clearings.

Snaking through the Gorge

Scratchboard, 16 x 12

If someone had been looking down upon us, I'm sure our narrow pathway must have looked like a flimsy black thread upon ruddy rocks. We had been plodding through this ravine for some time, a gully so narrow that it was a mere ten to fifteen wide in some places. The powerful loom of huge boulders on either side was an awe-inspiring sight. Looking up, it was very difficult to catch a glimpse of the blue sky. ❖ I had read that this gorge was not formed as a result of erosion—rather it had begun as a crack in the earth due to a big seismic shock. Then the persistent waters of Wadi Musa, with the help of relentless wind and sand, smoothed out the blunted edges. ❖ After about twenty minutes of hiking into the gorge, we came upon a clearing where the walls let up on their stranglehold. A Jordanian horseman, clad in a white tunic, rode his beautiful white steed past the red cliffs, lending a powerful contrast to the scene. ❖ I captured this mesmerizing vista on my drawing pad, noting the bright and dark contrasts. I also took a few pictures with my camera. It took me a couple of days to etch out the details on a black scratchboard.

An Age-Old History

The history of Petra is still cloaked in mystery. Bashar told us that Petra wasn't only about the Nabataeans; races spanning the full sweep of human civilization inhabited the area. Traces of Paleolithic man have been found on some of the higher mountain slopes, dating to about 10,000 B.C.E. Excavated remains of an entire Stone Age village have been discovered around this settlement.

As stunning as Al Khazneh was, I was also staggered by the enormity of Umm al-Biyara, the massive mountain dominating the center of Petra, whose summit housed a small village of the Edomite people who are mentioned in the Bible. During those times, probably as far back as the eleventh century B.C.E., the country was known as Edom.

The Nabataeans moved in around the sixth century B.C.E., launching a glorious period of building in their capital city. The place flourished for several centuries, but around the time of Christ, it was conquered by the Roman emperor Trajan. A series of devastating earthquakes in the late fourth century C.E. crippled the hydraulic system and brought buildings crumbling down. Years later, the city saw the rise of Islam and later endured the assaults of the Crusaders and the conquests of Saladin. Then it fell into a long period of silence until the explorer Johann Burckhardt came along.

FOOTLOOSE IN THE MOUNTAINS

I enjoyed many more and equally dramatic climbs along winding mountain trails to some of Petra's remote treasures. The Ad-Dayr monastery was an unfinished Nabataean tomb carved from a mountaintop high above the Petra basin. The High Place of Sacrifice was perhaps the most complete and best-preserved cultic altar and sacrificial complex, reminiscent of the hoary Biblical period. It took me over an hour to climb up to the obelisks around the altar. The processional way to this site and back is embellished by a series of stately temples, tombs, altars, fountains, and forts.

As evening approached, I realized it had been a tiring day, frequently carrying my son on the long hike. I now wended my way back on camel. My Bedouin charge was smiling snidely at my bumpy discomfiture as I struggled to keep my seat on the saddle.

When the Rocks Yawned Open!

Scratchboard and ink, 14 x 11

Gigantic red bastions towered on either side of us as we hiked into the cool Siq. Rocks with strange inscriptions from ancient eras punctuated the cliffs. ✤ At some places during the trek, the fissure of the Siq had narrowed down to a squishy ten feet. Suddenly everything changed — entirely. ✤ I stood transfixed, staring at the glory that had unfolded in front of me. This was truly one of the greatest travel moments in my life. Bashar had never told us what to expect after our long trek. ✤ "Is it raining in the mountains?" I had asked querulously just a few seconds earlier, definitely apprehensive as I imagined a flash flood roaring through the ravine. There had, in fact, been several floods, most recently in 1991, but most were unlike the catastrophic event in 1963 when several French tourists were swept away and drowned in the Siq. ✤ On this sunny morning, however, all fear was now gone. I hurried to get a better glimpse of the majesty hidden beyond the rock curtain. ✤ Ahead of me stood a massive, graceful Hellenistic beauty. Large groups of tourists from at least twenty countries, whose voices had raucously echoing through the narrow gorge just moments before, suddenly quieted in the surprise of the moment. ✤ The sun had found a way through the massive walls of rock to my right. Al-Khazneh was lit up by sunlight. A visitor dismounted from a camel, as a lone horseman stared at the endless red cliffs before him. ✤ I clicked a few photos, but didn't want to bother with a tripod to preserve so eternal a sight with so flimsy a medium. Much later I created this scene on scratchboard, using waterproof inks to fill in some of the hues, though they simply didn't measure up to nature's magical palette!

As I left those ruddy sands and gigantic cliffs, I realized that the most enduring monuments here were the ones carved by nature. I would never forget the eerie rock bridges, the towering rose-colored sand dunes, the daunting massifs that cast their shadows over the tiny crouch of human settlements below.

A full moon was lighting up the Jordanian sky. As my camel trudged towards our bus stand, I notice a sandstorm brewing, getting ready to bury many more secrets that had gathered with time. ✤

Help!: Al-Khazneh from a Ridge

Pen and ink, 14 x 11

We were allowed forty-five minutes to take in all this magnificent beauty. As the group busied itself with cameras and water bottles, I slipped away and began clambering up a goat path behind the Royal Tombs to get a loftier perspective of the Treasury. I had read about this secret pathway somewhere in a guidebook. ❖ Minutes into the climb, I reached a scary point of no return. I had lost the trail, and there was no one to be seen. I could still hear the sounds of civilization, but they were muted in the afternoon winds until they became only a faint and distant buzz. Somewhere below me, I could spot the fleck of camels, horses, and humans. ❖ To my immense relief, a group of Bedouin boys appeared from out of nowhere. They took me to a spot where I cautiously perched myself only a couple of feet away from what would have been a precipitous drop. ❖ The boys were urging me to go further up, but common sense set in. I clicked a couple of pictures, captured the scene in my memory, and very slowly made my way down using my rear end as a cushion until I had nearly destroyed my jeans. ❖ After what felt like a long and frightening interval, I finally made it back down to the ground. I spotted my tour group slowly assembling. I had never felt gladder to see them! ❖ I later created this pen and ink drawing in Tel Aviv.

Not far from the Roman Theater lie a series of tombs carved into the face of the mighty Jabal Al-Khubtha massif. Names have been given to these burial sites, which may have come out of a wanderer's fancy: the Silk Tomb, Corinthian Tomb, Three-Story Palace Tomb, and the Urn Tomb. This last was, in my opinion, the most impressive of all. ❖ The Urn Tomb was constructed sometime in the first century C.E. as a mausoleum for a powerful king of those times. The courtyard, adorned by a series of archways, was spectacular. In the upper story was a triclinium for a funerary banquet, and higher up were three niches that housed tombs out of reach of robbers' crowbars. ❖ I walked around and into the belly of this timeworn monument, eyeing the red rocks and their brilliantly colored undulations. I couldn't help wondering how skillful hands had carved these structures in the harsh desert landscape with such engineering accuracy. ❖ Later, in the haven of my studio, as I worked on this scratchboard from a photograph I had taken, I marveled all over again at the skill of those long-vanished artisans. It took me several days to complete a miniature 12 x 16 piece. I couldn't help adding my signature clad-in-white horseman in the foreground, though admittedly I didn't see him there.

Tributes to the Dead: The Royal Tombs

Scratchboard, 16 x 12

Two Camels:
Along the Colonnaded Street

Conté crayon, 11 x 14

I had hiked for nearly six hours, often stopping for my son, Anish, who was accidentally administered a shot of nighttime cold medicine in the morning. ❖ Our group came across what struck me as the recreation of an ancient scene: the bustle of downtown Petra. The city center is largely dominated by structures that reflect the glorious days of Nabataean power. However, where once stood monuments and bazaars were now assembled Arab peddlers hawking scarves, stone sculptures, and other interesting baubles. ❖ Far in the distance was what the locals call "Camel Rock," and as if by intended arrangement, in the foreground was an adamant camel resisting its owner's cajoling. Additionally, a sandstorm churned to my right, creating a surreal sight. I made a quick sketch on the spot, planning to add the details later in my Tel Aviv apartment. ❖ However, I needed to get there first. It was late afternoon and time to leave beautiful Petra. While crossing over to Jordan from Eilat was a smooth experience, the return to Israel was rather harrowing. ❖ My passport carried my South Indian sobriquet: first name followed by my father's name. Based on this traditional nomenclature, my first name was automatically my son's last name. Adding to the confusion, my son's passport photograph was long outdated, showing a baby scowling miserably at the camera, looking quite different from the genial five-year-old now gazing at a suspicious Israeli border official. ❖ Despite my explanation of South Indian naming conventions and pointing out the feeble resemblance between my son and his old photograph, the Israeli official was convinced I had kidnapped my charge. Between my English and his Hebrew, we engaged in a lengthy argument. He refused to let the bus pass until this issue was sorted out. After a tense hour-long exchange, we were allowed to depart albeit with a much lighter wallet. ❖ Welcomed by the hurrah of the other passengers, we began the drive back towards Tel Aviv.

Hurried Sketch: The Temple Mount behind the Western Wall, Jerusalem

Acrylic on paper, 11 x 14

I could not have been in a setting more revered and hallowed than the one that stood before me. The morning sun glistened upon the Dome of the Rock. The darkened silver dome of the al-Aqsa mosque peeked from above a wall. ❖ I perched myself high upon a stone parapet facing the Wailing Wall — a great vantage point, isolated from the incessant tromp of tourists. A blimp floated in the azure skies high above the distant chatter of pilgrims on the grounds below. ❖ Within seconds I heard footsteps behind me. Muttering curses directed at the species of tourists from anywhere and everywhere, I stayed focused on the outline I was drawing on my pad, then squeezed some tubes of paint onto my plastic palette. An instinct made me look up. I was surrounded by a posse of gun-toting Israeli soldiers, one of whom seemed very suspicious that I was carefully recreating a blueprint of the wall, as if for a murky reason. ❖ Remembering a sage piece of advice from a forebear about never looking a feral dog in the eye, I simply kept on with my artwork as if nothing unusual was happening. I hoped my shaking hand wouldn't betray me. ❖ Thirty suspenseful minutes later, I packed my bags and casually ambled away, at which point so did the soldiers. With my limited Hebrew lexicon I understood one of them to say something to the effect of: "Did we scare him away?" ❖ This piece is my reminder of that unforgettable day, and it still hangs in my studio in Chicago. Someone told me later that the harmless-looking blimp was in fact a surveillance balloon that closely monitors the sea of humanity below.

CHAPTER EIGHT

Israel ❖ Holy Land

Sanctums of Faith

It was like trying to hold eternity in the palm of my hand.

A year of living in and wandering through the Holy Land offered me stories of resolve, adventure, courage, altruism, and divinity. I had clambered up the slopes of Qumran and Masada, and envisioned the miracles at Capernaum and the sermons at Gethsemane. I had visited the Crusaders' bastions in Akko and Caesarea, and seen the sights of ancient Jaffa and Megiddo of Biblical times. Despite the threat of bullets and bombs, I had ventured into Jericho and Bethlehem, and paused to dip in the emerald waters of the Jordan River.

Yet nothing compared to the beauty of ancient Jerusalem, which some believe to be the greatest city in the world.

My wanderings in a city over six thousand years old took me into the veritable cradle of civilizations, one that over the centuries has been both illuminated by faith and rocked by strife. What were the secrets buried in this ancient capital of Judea that propelled modern generations to fight for a little strip of land just as generations of their forefathers had done during centuries of blood and battle?

Many a Sabbath weekend I would take off on my own explorations into a world of Canaanites and Israelites. I'd chance upon a pottery shard or walk the same muddy paths where one time walked warmongering Philistines and Ethiopians, mighty Egyptians and Assyrians, and resolute Greeks in search of loot. Here, too, the Romans had razed a massive temple to the ground, robbing a city of its splendor. Urged by the pope and afire with religious fervor, brave knights rode

Ramparts Timeless: The Tower of David, Jerusalem

Conté crayon, 12 x 16

Just across from Jaffa Gate stretches Jerusalem's Citadel and its handsome fortifications, the ruins of what some mistakenly believed to be the ancient palace of King David. An Ottoman-period minaret marks the signature setting of many a postcard that is available at gift stores throughout Israel. ❖ More than three thousand years of history have flashed by these ramparts shaped by the ancient Israelites, then the Arabs, the Mamluks, the Crusaders, and the Ottomans in centuries of conquest. An archaeological garden broke the monotony of the stony landscape that lay unfurled before me. ❖ A week before, on a nippy night, I had attended a vividly impressive sound-and-light show enacted against this magnificent backdrop. A Jewish acquaintance I was with told me a remarkable story. ❖ Twenty years before, an Orthodox Israeli man and his seven-year-old daughter were driving along a street not far from a dangerous area comprising a Palestinian stronghold. It wasn't unusual to hear the staccato of gunfire as the Israeli guards would open fire in retaliation to fiery Palestinian bombs that would rumble in the quiet of the desert. The little girl, with the friskiness of her age, opened the car door and was suddenly thrown out onto the dirt road. The panic-stricken father, fearing the worst, scrambled after her, only to see an old man from across the street pick up the injured girl and take her to his mean little dwelling. Here, the old man tended to her miraculously minor scrapes with the choicest medicaments he had and then carefully handed her back to her relieved father. ❖ The girl — now my acquaintance as well — recounted between sobs that the old man was a Palestinian Arab and had been killed by a stray bullet just two months after this extraordinary act of kindness. ❖ I sketched this desolate drama of stones in monochromatic crayon to depict the devastation that wars and conquest inevitably lead to. There was beauty in the intended arrangement of those humongous stone slabs, but just like the sad story I heard that lonely evening, no life to go with it.

in from distant lands, launching crusade after crusade to wrest these sites of Christian history from the Muslims, even though, paradoxically, herein also lay some of Islam's holiest spots.

It was entirely possible that I had walked the very path where a retinue of the devout, laden with offerings, began their trek towards the First or the Second Temple. Probably I had climbed up to the very site where King Solomon, King

David, or King Herod had come to inspect a construction of massive proportions.

Just as I had humbly faced the harsh reality of death in Varanasi, here in Jerusalem the sense of history was overwhelming. Here were lives unsung, soldiers fallen, and cultures unknown, impossible to record, forever buried in time. My pen, brush, and lens were feeble and inadequate tools with which to describe and convey what had taken millennia to both build and destroy. How could wood, lead, clay, fiber, and dye, even if coaxed into form by the most skilled craftsmen, let alone my unpracticed hand, accurately capture the powerful essence of this place and time?

It was a daunting challenge that I was thrilled to attempt.

Roaming the Holy Land with my paraphernalia, I found myself wondering how King Solomon, nearly three thousand years ago, managed to build a majestic temple that was later razed to the ground as a result of the wrath of Nebuchadnezzar. Later, with tremendous skill in engineering, the unrelenting Herod the Great built another massive structure on the same site. Thoughts of man-made feats led me to wonder what could rival Hezekiah's Tunnel, which brought water from a distant spring down a gentle gradient to slake the thirst of city denizens. And moving on, I would imagine in horror the Romans with their battle equipment launching an attack on the Second Temple, breaking down both walls and the spirit of the people of Jerusalem who so respected their own religion and values.

I followed the sojourns of that serene saint of Galilee who left an indelible mark upon the world. Disillusioned with the priestly politics of the temple, Jesus and his apostles walked these lands touching minds narrow and lives shallow. I reverently walked along the Via Dolorosa towards the Church of the Holy Sepulchre, where this great personage had chosen to end an era for the sake of his faith and people.

Striding under the many massive gates of Jerusalem, I spent several hours around the Mount of Olives, gazing at the sea of graves awaiting a messiah to deliver redemption one day. Upon a ridge by the Gihon Spring, the City of David rambles with its fortifications and ruins; once home to the ancient Jebusites, it had been transformed into a splendorous town where Israelites experienced centuries of both prosperity and destruction.

The Byzantine Empire banished Roman paganism to welcome Christianity, and then the Persians arrived. After that, the Arab conquest enveloped the Holy Land. The Crusaders marched in from Europe with one purpose: to regain a territory that their own religion was built on. They built castles and subterranean cities in Akko and Caesarea. The Mamluks vanquished the Crusaders, until finally, the Ottoman Empire held sway over these lands for generations.

In Jerusalem, walking from the Christian Quarter to the Armenian Quarter, from the Moroccan Quarter to the Muslim Quarter, I experienced a profound personal transformation. Gone were my preconceived dogmas and cultivated tenets, for in this broad palette of spirituality, there really is no room for one dogged belief or one obdurate faith. As the patriarchs and masters of old had preached, one's spirit is continually challenged to strengthen, and the old to tolerantly give way to the new.

This is how, through invasions and conversions, Judaism survived, much like the Hanukkah flame that kept itself alive in an ancient temple. Thus too was Christianity born, thriving with its many sects, unfazed by Muslim incursions. Against the backdrop of the Dome of the Rock, the muezzin call from the al-Aqsa mosque rends through the expanse of the Western Wall. It echoes through a monastery near the Golgotha where a Franciscan priest is preaching a compelling sermon.

On my first trip to Jerusalem, I was struck by the many religions, many sects, many places of worship, many people, and many views. On later visits, I began to realize that what seemed like many was truly but one. This city was simply a vast, monumental expression of human faith that transcended religion and dogmas.

Daunting Gates: Pathways for Ancient Chariots, Megiddo

Conté crayon, 12 x 16

Two hours from Tel Aviv we reached this ancient mound noted for its vertical archaeological cut that revealed the many civilizations forgotten in time. ❖ "Much of the archaeological work really began only in the mid-1900s," Eli remarked. "Initially, they started this work in sections, but found it easier to make a vertical cut instead through all the levels until they reached the bedrock." ❖ My guide and I walked along these deserted lanes which must have once buzzed with the activities of soldiers and horses, of ordinary townsfolk and markets. We came to a cylindrical hollow. It was a sunken grain silo, dating back to the eighth century B.C.E., that was about twenty-five feet deep, and then we came to the ruins of stables, probably from the reign of King Ahab in the ninth century B.C.E. ❖ The most intriguing part to me was simply walking into the massive gates of this ancient walled city. An enemy would have found it impossible to penetrate the defenses of these mighty casemate walls — stacks of stones with a gap between that could easily be filled with boulders and dirt during a siege or war. ❖ The sun was tormenting. Making a sketch, let alone coloring it, was nearly impossible under the oppressive heat and glare. My wife strayed into the scene, so I took a photo to establish proportion and to capture the sheer size of those walls and the resistance a marauder would contend with just to get past one set of gates into the fortified city. ❖ I later completed the sketch using a sepia Conté crayon on hot-pressed paper.

MEGIDDO: CRADLE OF CIVILIZATIONS

This is the very site of the Biblical Armageddon — that War of the End of the Days," Eli, my guide, exclaimed.

I stood in the ancient township of Megiddo, situated upon an embankment at the southern end of the Jezreel Valley. In such an utter state of ruin, I could discern only clusters of stones and rubble, but a trained archaeologist could see a sprawl of altars and stables, massive roads along which chariots had trundled, and luxurious palaces and ritual grounds dating back more than five thousand years.

Looking at my map, it was clear that this fortified township must have been a strategic hub along the Via Maris — the ancient trade route from Egypt to Damascus and beyond, connecting cities as old as Ur and Babylon. The scene of many a bloody battle for control throughout the ages, it wasn't surprising to me that a vertical archaeological cut had uncovered twenty-five layers of civilization dating from 5000 to 400 B.C.E. (left).

"Timeless Megiddo is even mentioned in the written records of the Egyptians," Eli said. Hieroglyphics on the wall of the Karnak Temple in Luxor recount the battle that the Pharaoh Tutmose III fought here in the fourteenth century B.C.E. Legend runs that the King had chosen the most difficult point to penetrate its defenses, since he knew that his Canaanite opponents would least expect an attack from this point.

Several rulers took control of this town before King David eventually captured it for the Israelites. Megiddo reached its heyday in the later reigns of Solomon and Ahab, yet amidst the cacophony of stones before me, it was hard to believe that it must have been one of the most beautiful cities of those times.

It was late afternoon when I finished my tour of the massive stables and what had once been a large silo. But what remains most prominent in my mind about Megiddo is its underground water tunnel dating back to the ninth century B.C.E. I went down a steep flight of stone stairs into the dark depths of a passageway, part of the ancient water system of King Ahab's time. A large shaft had been drilled through more than a hundred feet of rock, connecting to an underground tunnel that snaked more than two hundred feet to a hidden spring just outside the city. During a siege, the women of Megiddo tiptoed from their fortress along this passage to draw water for their daily cooking.

As I emerged from these dank depths onto a grassy outlet in the sunlight, I realized this egress would have once been cleverly camouflaged.

Intrigued by it all, I would have enjoyed learning about those twenty-five civilizations now forgotten in time. Alas, their tales are buried somewhere in the rubble.

JAFFA: SPLENDOR BY THE SEA

The shore looked colorful that sunny morning, with painted boats bobbing in the waves. A clump of half-submerged boulders could mark the spot where Andromeda was saved by mighty Perseus from sacrifice to a fearsome sea monster.

I stood in Biblical Jaffa, one of the oldest working harbors in the world today (right). Heavily in use before King Solomon the Wise came to power, Jewish pilgrims landed their ships here, in anticipation of their long trek to Jerusalem to visit their great temple.

A mere three miles from Tel Aviv, Jaffa is a town of opposites. Old Jaffa is full of ancient buildings and quaint streets and a busy port, while the newer city is lit up with restaurants and clubs. The name "Yafo" is derived from the Hebrew "Japheth," the son of Noah who,

Done for the Day!: Full Moon Night, Jaffa

Scratchboard, 11 x 14

Thursday evening brought a full moon, and I briskly walked along the bustling promenade to Jaffa from my sea-facing rental apartment on Trumpeldor Street. A cool breeze pushed me along the palm-fringed coastline as I watched the sea play against the rocks. ❖ Past the Ottoman clock tower, the souvenir shops, and the countless Arab bakeries that marked the beginning of Old Jaffa, a winding pedestrian walkway took me to the ancient monuments of this township. Curious porches and quaint buildings were everywhere. Most appealing to me were the little art and jewelry shops tucked in the narrow streets. The loom of St. Peter's Monastery is all-pervading in Old Jaffa; its bell tower seemed to follow me into every nook and cranny of the place. ❖ I walked past many narrow lanes towards the port, noticing a maritime mosque where a prayer was in progress. Along the shore of this ancient port, I imagined armies of yore in lusty conquests and pilgrims in devotion disembarking on these shores. ❖ I found a quiet spot and came upon this charming scene. Moonbeams sloped down on the lapping waters and all was still. Suddenly, from one of these buildings a fisherman called out to his partner who was docking his boat. Long years ago, this could have been a Turk or a Crusader clad in white calling it a day after a long journey. ❖ Standing under a streetlamp, I sketched this scene in pencil and months later recreated it on scratchboard, which best conveyed the feel of that velvety night, the silvery moon, and the quiet hush of the scene.

according to legend, established this township after the floods. Centuries ago the famed Lebanese cedars for Solomon's Temple landed here; it was during the King's reign that it really became the famed seaport of Palestine.

I enjoyed the vista of quaint buildings and the sunny sprawl of streets and monasteries. Once occupied by the Canaanites, the Egyptians conquered this town in the fifteenth century B.C.E., their soldiers taking the city by surprise by hiding within consignments being transported to the local market. Jaffa's later history was marked by bloody wars as it was successively conquered by the Arabs, the Crusaders, the Ottomans, and the Mamluks.

As I walked towards Jaffa along the seaside promenade from Tel Aviv, it was hard to grasp the depth of history in these placid stones. Now a bustling town replete with art galleries and souvenir shops, a lot of tourists begin their Holy Land pilgrimage here, with their first day's halt at Tel Aviv. Stalls were full of hungry tourists jostling to taste the Israeli fare of pita bread with hummus followed by falafel. Eager Japanese students wielded their cameras with their usual dexterity.

As I turned to watch the sunset, the pale yellow sun was sinking against the silhouette of St. Peter's Church and all the buildings of ancient Jaffa. A few fishing boats were idling in the lap of the sea waves.

I wondered how this place must have looked with loads of cedar from Lebanon landing in these very docks, in preparation for a great temple project in Jerusalem. A blaring horn from a large motorboat broke my musings.t

QUMRAN: IN SEARCH OF THE SACRED SCROLLS

In 1947, before the partition of Palestine, three Bedouin boys were grazing their sheep high upon the sandy slopes. One lobbed a stone up a hollow and heard a clink. Fearfully climbing up the rocks, they saw a cave and drew near, where they came upon a row of old, lidded jars.

Over the next few years, archaeologists began their excavations on the site, and more than twenty-one caves (pages 134-5) were discovered with numerous jars containing scrolls depicting the history of a civilization gone by. A few different types of scrolls were discovered, including the books of the Bible and various sectarian works describing contemporary life. One of these works lists in detail the treasures of the Holy Temple of Jerusalem, which were stashed away all over Judea after the Roman conquest. Another describes the strife between the Essenes and Romans.

"A group of two hundred ultra-orthodox Essenes worked tirelessly to scribe the Bible for posterity," my guide, Eli, told me as we drove to this ancient archeological site. I could make out many hollows upon the sandy mounds as we neared the area. A breakaway sect of the Jewish community, the Essenes disapproved of the religious practices of Jerusalem and withdrew into the eerie wilderness of the Judean desert. Harsh Qumran was their colony, far removed from the hubbub of Jerusalem, away from the persecution of the Romans. This celibate community lived here between 130 B.C.E. and 70 C.E., tilling land, making pottery, tending sheep, and working on the now-famous Dead Sea Scrolls.

While inside the caves, Eli said, "You would see much about Qumran if you made a visit to the Israel Museum in Jerusalem where the Dead Sea scrolls are now preserved."

A week later I did exactly that, for among the rubble of Qumran, it was difficult to picture all this vividly. Gone were the secret Essenes, their frenetic scribing, and their ritualistic fervor.

Only those lone caves stood as a testament to a tempestuous past.

Vulture in the Skies: Caves of Sacred Scrolls, Qumran

Watercolor, 12 x 16

It was a chilly December morning as my sprightly seventy-six-year-old guide, Eli, trundled his van along the Tel Aviv roads. Driving past Jerusalem and then Jericho, I noticed the landscape change dramatically, from one of cultivated lushness to the harshness of the Judean desert. Around sixty miles from Tel Aviv, we approached the ruddy mounds of Qumran, laced by the salty Dead Sea. ❖ The site lay upon a plateau. Opposite, in the cliffs, were some of the famous scroll caves. In fact, I could see the much-photographed Cave 4, just as the Bedouins had found it. ❖ From an ancient watchtower, I faced the blue swath that was the Dead Sea. Below me was an elaborate cistern system that ensured a good supply of water in the barren desert. I walked into the ruins of what must have been a scriptorium, imagining zealous amanuenses engrossed in their holy project. ❖ High above the barrenness, a lone vulture shrieked. There was nothing in the landscape save the undulating drapery of the harsh rocks. As the huge bird winged in the cloudy skies, I pictured how Qumran's people would have lived in such harsh conditions, alone, driven by their beliefs, until the Roman invasion forever snuffed out a community and its secrets. ❖ I positioned myself upon a sandy ledge watching the wadi to my left. All around me were rocky mounds as far as the eye could see, mottled with specks that were countless slits in the rocks, some probably holding more stories waiting to be told. The vulture crisscrossed above me several times, probably wondering why a living thing would pause that long upon the rocks. ❖ Several wet-on-wet washes with the use of a dry brush on rag paper recreated the atmosphere of the moment.

Caesarea: A Maritime Marvel

Ancient Caesarea is located in northwest Israel, lapped by the turquoise waters of the Mediterranean Sea (right). Two thousand years ago this was a massive harbor city built by Herod the Great upon the remains of an older Phoenician settlement. In the centuries to follow, this city rose to be the Roman capital of Palestine, a status it held for almost six hundred years.

"Long ago, the harbor was capable of docking more than three hundred ships," my guide, Eli, said. He picked up a shard of a clay vessel and passed it along to me.

Over twenty-five hundred years ago, Phoenician traders built a town by the sea called Strato's Tower. This place was once conquered by the Romans, gifted to Cleopatra, and eventually handed over to the appointed Jewish king, Herod, in 37 B.C.E. It was then that a nondescript seaside town attained world renown. King Herod constructed one of the greatest ports and cities in history, naming it after the Roman emperor Augustus Caesar. As I held a piece of history in my hands, I pictured pilgrims thronging to temples and noisy theaters and markets lining the wide roads within this city's fortified ramparts.

Thriving during the Byzantine period, the city was occupied by the Arabs and then the Crusaders who landed their huge ships here, further strengthening those ramparts. In the thirteenth century, the ruthless Mamluks razed this splendid city to the ground, burying it in obscurity for hundreds of years. Caesarea was later captured by the Ottomans, who in the nineteenth century settled Bosnian refugees here.

It was early evening as the sun shone down on the thirty-five-hundred-seat amphitheater built in the time of King Herod. Walking towards the fortified Medieval City, I passed the ruins of the king's lavish seaside palace.

History seemed to breathe from every stone in this town. The apostle Paul lay imprisoned here for a couple of years, and Peter preached the Gospel here to a Roman centurion named Cornelius. The recently discovered Pilate Stone revealed that the same Pontius Pilate who sanctioned the crucifixion of Jesus governed these lands.

It was getting dark as we turned the van around, ready to head back. The crescent moon beamed down on the aqueduct as restless waves crashed upon the shore. The unyielding march of time had spared nothing; all that was left of Herod's majestic city and its glitter was, alas, mere memories and sad ruin.

Boy Exploring an Aqueduct: Caesarea

Watercolor, 11 x 14

We trudged for hours along the deserted lanes of this medieval city that once teemed with soldiers and horses, people and markets. By evening I was completely drained, but not my guide, who said that there was one more spectacle worth seeing just a short drive away: the great Roman aqueduct. ❖ I could see the snaky stretch of a stone structure that fetched the waters from the hidden Shuni springs in misty Mount Carmel, more than ten miles away. In a gradual gradient, the waters trickling in three channels were held aloft by sturdy Roman arches, a fantastic feat in stone that had stood its ground against the elements. These channels fed into pools and pipes that then slaked the thirst of the city's populace. ❖ As I took in the span of the structure, I couldn't help admiring the engineering marvel that extended as far as the eye could see. At that instant, Anish, then six, who had gotten used to watching us seek out pottery shards and shiny porcelain, began his own explorations. ❖ His diminutive frame against such an expansive backdrop propelled me to sketch it all. ❖ I used watercolor on cold-pressed paper to capture the effect of the sunlight upon curved arches and ruddy bricks in this sandy setting.

The Afternoon Service: View of an Ancient Harbor, Caesarea

Watercolor, 18 x 24

A brilliant feat accomplished by Herod's Roman architects, this unique marvel by the seashore, Caesarea, was also an artist's delight. ❖ That wintry morning, the colors and the contrasts were everywhere. A lazy sun had just pierced through a gray cloudbank, magically lighting up the sky behind this setting. Ahead of me stretched the swath of an ancient Crusader city, flavored with stones from the many centuries that preceded the knights' conquest. Even from where I stood it was easy to make out ancient Byzantine columns embedded within the Crusader ruins, as well as stones from Crusader ramparts that had been ruthlessly broken down for constructing Ottoman mosques. ❖ The minaret of the Bosnian mosque stuck out in the background as a crowd of pilgrims streamed out after a morning service. I imagined the bustle of hundreds of skilled builders and divers working on creating those huge breakwaters, lowering mammoth stones into the sea. Colossal statues may have lined this entrance to the city, and a gigantic lighthouse may have guided ships to safety. ❖ I met Ari, an archaeologist from New York, who was unearthing more secrets from the complex in the foreground. He showed me several artifacts from his recent exploration and commented that few visitors to the Holy Land really appreciate Caesarea for the architectural marvel it was. ❖ It wasn't until a year later that I picked up the largest block of watercolor paper I could lay my hands on and finished this piece with several washes.

Pilgrims in Prayer: Church of the Nativity, Bethlehem

Acrylic on board, 16 x 20

There was no time to stand and stare. Hundreds of buses and cars were belching out families and friends who had traveled thousands of miles to glimpse the homeland of someone who changed the history of the world forever. ❖ The Church of the Nativity marks the traditional site of the cave where Christ was born. The main entrance to this enormous "citadel" church was through a small door. Two other openings had been blocked off by the Crusaders who wanted to deter marauders from riding in here on their horses. Later, during the Ottoman period, the entrance was made even smaller to prevent looters from driving their carts inside. ❖ I made a quick sketch. Then I noticed a German tour group seemingly intrigued by the clanging bells in the white turret above. It had been a rather cloudy afternoon, but now the sun had come out and the scene was transformed in a trice. Sunbeams touched down upon the spires, lighting up the skies. This in turn cast an eerie glow upon the polished stones by the church entrance, broken only by the shadow of the turret. I could see a distant throng squeezing their way in through the narrow entrance. ❖ My bulky camera with its numerous and complex settings was useless in trying to capture a scene that lasted but a few seconds. Instead I recorded this moment in my memory. In the power of such an amazing moment, reality gives way to a state of artistic expression in which what one sees in a special way is what matters, not what one knows is there. ❖ When I got to the entrance, I had to bend down, laden with my art paraphernalia, to fit through it. Someone mentioned that this was aptly known as the Door of Humility.

BETHLEHEM: BIRTH OF A RELIGION

I was lost in the cobblestone streets of a legendary Palestinian township that lay just six miles shy of Jerusalem. I wasn't alone here in Manger Square, for there were thousands of the devout from far-flung nations who had flocked to the land where Jesus Christ was born.

Unknown to many, Bethlehem is as sacred to the Jews as it is to the Christians. It was through King David that Bethlehem gained its initial importance. Years later, the Roman emperor Caesar Augustus ordered a census of all Roman provinces, which is what brought the couple Mary and Joseph from Nazareth to their native city. With no room in the crowded inns, they took refuge in a grotto, thus creating a new chapter in Biblical history.

For a couple of centuries following Jesus' death, Bethlehem was a center of paganism until Christendom gained ground with the rise of the Byzantine Empire in the fourth century. Emperor Constantine ordered the construction of monumental churches to commemorate three major events of Jesus' life; one of them was a church enshrining the scene of the Nativity in Bethlehem (left).

If stones could speak, one of the oldest churches in the world would narrate its long history of resilience, not just against the marauding forces of another religion, but also against thefts, natural calamities, and clashes of people possessing different Christian faiths. The revolt of the Samaritans in the early part of the sixth century left the ancient church badly damaged. Emperor Justinian caused a new one to be erected in its place, which has survived today despite centuries of turmoil.

When the Persians overran Palestine in the early 600s, they spared the church. A later Arab invasion turned bloody, monasteries were razed and their occupants massacred, but the Church of the Nativity was respected. The Crusaders came in 1099, turning the church into an impregnable fortress. As Bethlehem grew wealthy from an influx of pilgrims, the walls and floors of the church were covered with marble and mosaic.

After a few more incursions, the Christians repossessed the church towards the end of the seventeenth century, but members of numerous sects often clashed with each

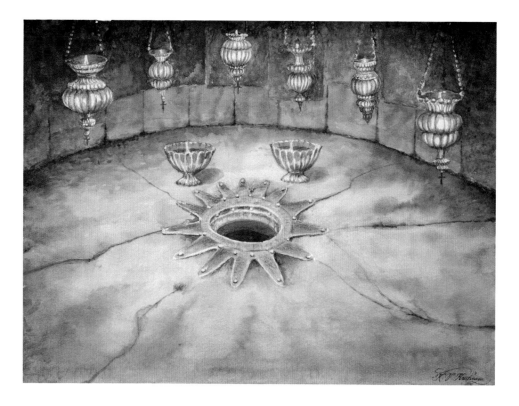

Hic de Virgine Maria Jesus Christus Natus Est: Bethlehem

Watercolor on hot-pressed paper, 11 x 14

In the darkness of the grotto lit only by the flicker of oil lamps lay that revered symbol of Christianity: the Star of Nativity. In the center of this gleaming silver circle is inscribed the words: Hic de Virgine Maria Jesus Christus Natus Est. Here, Jesus Christ was born of Virgin Mary. ❖ It was a solemn moment witnessing this emotional scene. The devout from far and wide had just fulfilled their single-minded goal, that of catching a glimpse of the spot where a savior had been born, one who would someday endure the sins of humanity. Many broke down, while others closed their eyes in silent prayer or bent down in front of the altar to kiss that magical star. ❖ It was hard to find a spot from where I could snap a quick photo, and I eventually had to nudge my way forward. Within the curtained enclosure of the altar, an array of lamps suspended from chains flickered in front of marbled walls, cloaked in what seemed like ancient Persian hangings. In the center of the flow, a multi-pointed silver star gleamed. ❖ I later sketched the scene and proceeded to paint this in watercolor, ignoring those finer details and symbols that are an important part of religion and faith. Later, I realized to my dismay that I had finished and signed a work with a star that was short of three points. The actual star has fourteen points, symbolizing, some say, the genealogy of Jesus, which encompasses three periods with fourteen generations each. ❖ Altering any work of watercolor is a challenge. Worse, I had painted this on light, hot-pressed paper, so rubbing off the paint with paper towels would inevitably destroy three days of dedicated work. Boldly, I painted a white acrylic coat, masking my eleven-point star, and layered several washes to create a star with its correct fourteen points. ❖ I couldn't have rested knowing I had incorrectly depicted something so deeply symbolic.

other. Violence was rife during the regime of the Ottoman Turks. The church even withstood a massive earthquake and a great fire.

With the jostle of eager pilgrims, it became quite congested within the cave. A narrow flight of stairs led me down to the Grotto of the Nativity, controlled by the Greek Orthodox, where it is believed Jesus was born. Marking the spot is the famous, glimmering silver Star of Nativity (left), kissed by countless pilgrims. Across from it is a recess where Jesus had lain in a manger.

Later in the evening, I walked past colorful markets to visit the Tomb of Rachel, one of Judaism's most sacred shrines and also revered by Muslims and Christians.

As our bus wended its way towards Tel Aviv, gun-toting soldiers were inspecting every vehicle that passed through the border checkpost. The place was noisy: traffic jams, honking cars, angry passengers breaking into fistfights. It was far removed from that quiet night seen by the Magi many centuries ago.

NAZARETH: IN THE LAND OF JESUS

Nazareth marks a major chapter in Christianity." Moshe, my guide, pointed out the colorful Gilead mountains of Jordan from across the lake of Galilee. "It was Mary's hometown. Jesus spent many of his childhood years in what was then a poor village."

We were driving towards an age-old place predating Christianity. Now it is one of the most populous Arab townships in Israel.

It was a noisy Saturday morning. Driving by modern buildings and the offices of several software companies, I witnessed an altercation between a group of Palestinian youths and some Israeli guards at a checkpoint. Could this really be, I wondered, one of the holiest shrines of Christianity?

Past the muezzin's call, I came across several of the many monasteries and convents tucked away throughout this modern town. Believed to be the home of Mary and Joseph before the birth of Jesus, many of Nazareth's attractions were located in the older part of town.

Like many ancient sites in the Holy Land, history was buried here among layers of

Peace in the Clatter:
Sunset at Nazareth

Acrylic, 16 x 20

A two-hour drive north from Tel Aviv brought me to the ancient city of Nazareth, one of Israel's largest Arab towns. Going by the billboards I saw, the local Arab population must know their city as "en-Nasra." ❖ The place was bustling with tourists as well as with vendors peddling their colorful wares. I stopped for lunch and ordered one of my favorite dishes: hummus generously slathered with chickpeas and pine nuts, garnished with paprika, along with a couple of spicy falafels perched upon my plate. ❖ I came across this charming view in early evening. In the mad bustle of Nazareth, the Basilica of the Annunciation stood out, nestled in a forest of green. Everything else was concrete and stone — shops and apartments, mosques and churches — and busy roads with honking cars crisscrossing the scene. On the roof of a building, an exciting football game was in full swing. ❖ This was truly a land of contrast — the old cheek by jowl with the new. Against the ancient, majestic basilica was the frenzy of a city roiling in concrete clutter. Here was this restful peace of a spectacular sunset upon the riot of humanity below. ❖ I sketched this and took several photographs. What was striking to me was the palette of colors in the skies, and the exhalations of a city only accentuated the effect. I was peculiarly struck by the mosque in the foreground rubbing shoulders with a nearby church; this in a tenuous land split by faiths and strife. At that moment a Bedouin shepherd stumbled into the golden canvas with an eager sheep taking the lead. ❖ I decided to use a canvas board and slow-drying acrylic colors to capture the scene.

eras and kingdoms, beliefs and controversies, buildings and rubble. An ancient altar marking what was believed to be Mary's childhood home had been transformed by the Byzantines into a Church of the Annunciation, commemorating the prophesy of the angel Gabriel to Mary that she would be the mother of Jesus. A later Crusader-era church built upon the Byzantine ruins was destroyed by the Mamluk incursion in 1260, reducing the flow of Christian pilgrims to a trickle.

In the early 1600s, the Franciscans purchased this land, reestablishing a Christian presence in this town where Jesus spent his youth prior to commencing his ministry in Capernaum. The modern basilica was built in 1969. Past bronze doors, I walked inside to a riot of colors from the stained-glass windows splayed brilliantly against bare stone. I was most intrigued by the mural collection depicting Mary and the baby Jesus, which had been donated by Catholic communities from all around the world. A piece from faraway Japan had Mother Mary's ornamentations made of exotic pearls.

Just as in any ancient town, there were innumerable sights steeped in faiths and beliefs. Christianity's ancient footprints led me to St. Joseph's Church, which marked the spot where Jesus' father had his carpentry workshop, and to St. Gabriel's Church, where some believe the Angel originally made his prophecy when Mary had come to draw water from the gurgling spring nearby.

Through a maze of steep and narrow winding lanes, I walked up Casa Nova Street into a lively Arab market. A light rain pattered upon the cobblestones of what must have been a humble village of a few citizens in Jesus' time, but was now a fractious Silicon Valley of sixty thousand, teeming with all the clatter of a typical weekend.

To me Nazareth stood as an example of how everything transforms with time. In all that honk of traffic and shouts of the denizens, an image of a sleepy town with just the rasps of a saw or thuds of a hammer from Joseph's workshop would be sounds from a very distant past.

The White Synagogue: Capernaum

Scratchboard, 14 x 11

Having driven from Tel Aviv to Capernaum, I had, unbeknownst to me, suddenly descended more than 650 feet below sea level. ❖ This ancient biblical village was abandoned more than a thousand years ago. A beautiful fourth-century synagogue stood resolutely over the ruins of what must have been a vibrant colony. ❖ Its white limestone structure stood in stark contrast to the grayish-black basalt stones scattered around. If this was indeed built upon an older first-century synagogue from Jesus' time, I was standing where the sage preached his sermons, converting the obdurate unbelieving and enlightening the doubtful. ❖ Inside the synagogue, I was struck not just by the contrast of black and white, but also by the stillness and quiet in what was once a place of animated discussions. Lined by tall columns and intricate friezes, there seemed to be a distinct Roman influence to this handsome edifice. I was especially captivated by the array of carved columns interspersed by broken pillars that lay in sad destruction. I could only think of the many prayers said here and the many lips that had kissed these walls in fervent worship. ❖ Long shadows fell upon the structure, lending a curious mixture of black and white, light and shade. ❖ I snapped a few photographs for details, but focused on my pencil sketch for capturing the interplay of light upon this monument. Later I used rugged scratchboard scraped with a #11 X-Acto scalpel.

CAPERNAUM: MASTER OF MIRACLES

Little girl, get up!" pronounced the white-robed saint to the child who had died before he could reach her bedside. Legend runs that upon hearing this command — "Talitha, koum!" in Aramaic — the dead girl mysteriously awoke from her eternal slumber.

The sun beamed down onto the remains of an ancient synagogue, peculiar with its stark whiteness against the black basalt ruins all around it. It struck me that the hush around this ornate fourth-century place of worship surely stood in contrast to the ceaseless bustle the streets here were used to when, long ago, Jesus preached his sermons in the synagogue that now lay beneath this structure.

I was right there, by the hushed ripples of the Sea of Galilee in Capernaum, one of the holiest of Christian lands. This was the place of Jesus' ministry and his apostles and disciples, the location of miracles performed by a man held divine: quelling a storm, exorcising demons, curing the incurable, even raising bodies from the dead.

During the Christian and fourth-century Byzantine periods, Capernaum prospered, its residents engaged in trade, fishing, and agriculture. Though the town's known history goes back only to the second century B.C.E., archaeologists believe this place must have existed long before those times. It would have been a busy border town along the Via Maris, the grand highway leading to the glitter of Damascus and lands further beyond.

I stood by a modern church, under which were the ruins of a small colony. This house of Saint Peter must have seemed enormous in its day, with several rooms around an expansive courtyard. A hive of activity then, the chants of sermons and the voices of its congregation, would have echoed within these walls.

During this tranquil interlude soothed by a soft breeze from the Sea of Galilee, it wasn't hard to envision this village during the time of Jesus, a place to which tired travelers walked for miles, eager to hear inspiring words of a saint — if only to come out soothed and transformed.

AKKO: GATEWAY TO SACRED LANDS

But for the clang of the clock tower and the buzz of motorboats, this could have been a scene from medieval times. Even after reading my guidebook over and over again, I found it impossible to keep straight in my mind the many rulers hailing from assorted kingdoms who had ceaselessly struggled

Light from the Clouds: The Mount of Beatitudes, Capernaum

Watercolor, 11 x 14

We were headed from Capernaum to the shrine marking the spot where Jesus had preached his famed Sermon on the Mount. Nearly two thouand years ago, a throng of devotees who had come from far and wide had congregated here to listen to their saint speak. We had just driven past ancient Tabgha, site of the ancient Church of the Multiplication, where some believe Jesus had miraculously fed thousands from a few loaves of bread and some fish. ❖ "There!" my guide, Eli, suddenly exclaimed with a flourish. "Behold the Mount of Beatitudes!" ❖ At first blush, I couldn't make out anything distinctive except for the tranquility of the scene. I eyed what seemed like a vast hilly meadow cloven by a narrow road. A sea of wildflowers bloomed ahead of me, as if to celebrate this moment. ❖ On top of the grassy promontory, though, was a glistening building upon which the late-afternoon sun was beaming down. As I later discovered, the Church of the Beatitudes was built in an octagonal shape to commemorate the eight Beatitudes that Jesus preached upon this hill. ❖ It was truly an inspirational moment that needed to be preserved in art. I sketched this scene using several layers of watercolor applied on cold-pressed paper, focusing particularly on capturing the luminous cloudbank.

Spice and Color:
View of the Harbor, Akko

Watercolor, 15 x 20

I had taken a ninety-minute train ride that morning from Tel Aviv, which brought me to the picturesque Crusader town of Akko, also known as Acre, set against the Mediterranean Sea. ❖ Mesmerized by the heady smell of spices and seawater, I stood gazing at the harbor of one of the oldest cities in the world. Here was history on a display-board setting — dappled with age-old mosques and churches, monasteries, Crusader fortresses and tunnels esoteric, colorful Turkish baths and synagogues. I keenly felt their powerful medieval mystique. ❖ To my right I could see the mosque of Sinan Basha and several other shrines of worship in the canvas of that setting. The Clock Tower loomed to the left, but the dials were noticeably missing that particular morning. An array of boats added an element of colorful clutter to the waterscape; the reflections in the water were truly as interesting as the composition upon it. In the distance was the bustle of a lively marketplace and a boat laden with a consignment of spices docking at the pier. As if on cue, another came chugging up. It was named Holbein — as if after an Old Master whose art I admired, as well as the brand name of the paints I was carrying with me. I took several photographs and noted the play of colors, values and contrasts on my sketchpad. ❖ I painted this scene some months later on a 140-pound cold-pressed paper, scratching out the reflections with a paper blade.

Knight with a Sword: Akko

Watercolor, 9 x 12

The Ottoman-era streets of Old Akko with their teeming souks looked truly charming as sunlight dappled upon shop awnings. After a dash of tasty tahini, I walked past stalls that peddled colorful spices and souvenir shops stocked with the most curious objects I could never have ordered from a catalog! ❖ Even more fascinating, a fantastic world lay underneath these cobblestones. I noticed a group of archaeologists working to uncover an enormous underground city that had been built by the Crusaders. The Knights of St. John had originally been established here in the eleventh century C.E. to care for the sick of Jerusalem. They even built their own hospital, but the organization soon became more interested in political power. ❖ I explored this seemingly endless subterranean world of dining rooms and pillared hallways, dungeons and an elaborate sewage system that crisscrossed under the entire city. Somewhere here, Richard the Lionheart may have entertained his royal guests from France. ❖ I could also imagine knights clad in mail and armor, exiting the city in a swift march through an escape tunnel that connected the seaport to the ancient fortress, even as invading forces were penetrating the main defenses. They died fighting for the bigger cause — the liberation of the Holy Land. ❖ At one point, my son's movements caught my eye. With only his little plastic shark for protection, he looked awed, even overwhelmed by the enormity of the vaulted ceilings and the somberness of the place. Yet behind him, the morning sun had found expression through the arched entrance, lightening up the mood of the moment. ❖ I later painted in the brilliance of the light through several watercolor washes of New Gamboge and Raw Sienna on cold-pressed paper.

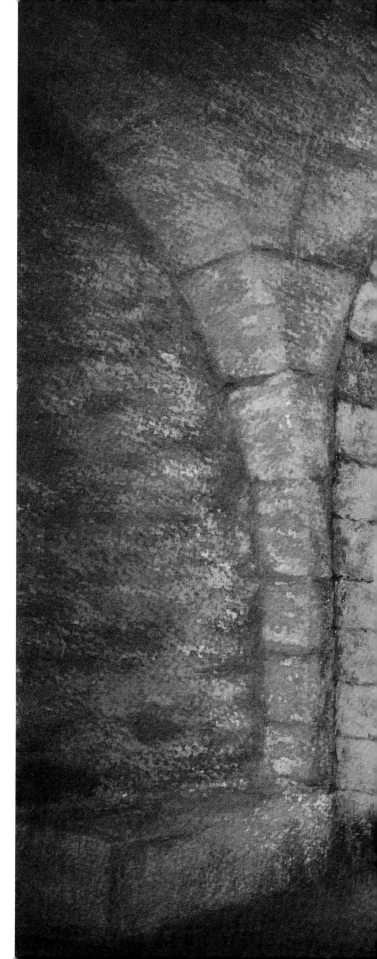

over the centuries to hold suzerainty over this exceptionally well-positioned seaport. In addition, anyone who controlled Akko would surely hold sway over holy Jerusalem, a mere one hundred miles away.

Long ago in the fifteenth century B.C.E., the pharaohs of Egypt knew of this city that had preceded them, and the ancient Greeks recounted how the invincible Hercules often visited this place in search of curative herbs. Originally settled by Assyrians, Akko was later conquered by Alexander the Great, the Romans, and a succession of Byzantine rulers until the Arabs took over this bustling seaport in the seventh century C.E. The Crusaders then followed with their shining weaponry, arriving in their ships from distant Genoa, Pisa, and Venice, ousting the Arabs and rebuilding Akko into a crossroad between Europe and the Holy Land. Muslims proudly recall how Saladin, sultan of Egypt and Syria, ruled over the Holy Land until the Crusaders reclaimed the city in their Third Crusade. Alas, the city fell into ruin when the marauding Mamluks pillaged the city in 1291. A few hundred years later, the Ottoman Turks gained power, holding it from the sixteenth century on, until British troops landed here in 1918. Britain later ceded control when Israel was formed in 1948.

As my train sped towards Tel Aviv, I recalled my stop at the Mansion of Bahji, the house of Baha'u'llah, the founder of the Baha'i faith. Consigned to the dreaded dungeons of Akko by the Ottoman Turks for practicing a faith that espoused openness to all religions, Baha'u'llah spent his final years in this house, preaching his faith. How apt it now seemed, when thinking about the city's fabulously variegated history.

MASADA: FORTRESS IN THE DESERT

I was upon a lone mesa in an arid terrain by the Dead Sea. Nearly two thousand years ago, the stony walls of this desert fortress likely resounded with the soulful oration of a besieged leader as he eyed the Romans from the ramp below while they launched their final assault. Nearly a thousand Zealots and their families were hopelessly cornered. This left them with but one choice: martyrdom by mass suicide.

This once-impregnable fortress in Masada (pages 156-7), perched thirteen hundred feet high atop jagged tawny cliffs, was indeed the scene of one of the most poignant moments of patriotism in history. King Herod, who ruled under Roman patronage, built many palaces, but his winter residence in Masada was different. Propelled by fears of a Jewish revolt, this three-layered bastion had been constructed as a place of refuge from rebellion. Replete with massive walls, storehouses, and cisterns, this was luxury in the harsh desert environment.

After the destruction of the Second Temple in Jerusalem in the first century C.E., Masada became a refuge for Jewish Zealots who fled with their families. Herod's protected palace became a lively colony of rebels, with synagogues, granaries, and ritual baths all within its impenetrable walls.

In 73 C.E., the Roman army finally laid siege to Masada. Fifteen thousand armed soldiers surrounded the hill for seven long months, and the frustrated Romans eventually began constructing an embankment upon the western slope. The Jewish warriors realized there was no way out. Men slew their own kith and kin to preserve their honor. The Romans then charged into the fort only to be met with a deathly silence. They discovered a cowering group of women and children who had somehow managed to save themselves from a gory fate.

"The Romans may have conquered the fortress," my guide Eli said, "but they couldn't conquer the people."

From atop Masada, I could see the snake of the charming Moab Mountains of Jordan and the remains of Roman camps dotting the skyline. The Dead Sea was a bejeweled glitter in the far distance. A lone crow settled raucously upon a wall near the area where the Romans had breached the bastion, near the very spot where courageous lives were bartered for passion and dignity that unforgettable day. ❖

Bastion of the Resolute, Masada

Conté crayon, 14 x 18

Ignoring the luxury of a cable car, I took the longer "Snake Path" that winds more than an hour's walk up the cliffs to the fortress. The climb was rewarding, and I enjoyed watching the sun rise over the gorgeous Moab Mountains. ❖ Reaching the top that warm morning, I met a group of young Israeli soldiers walking solemnly around these stones. I later learned from my guide that Masada stood as a symbol for Israel patriotism and as a fervent reminder that this nation's defenses should never be breached again as had happened that unfortunate day. ❖ All around us, the remains of a fortress sprawled in the sun. Inexplicably, there was a pile of catapult stones, each a foot and a half in diameter. ❖ I could imagine Roman legionaries armed to the teeth with their massive battle equipment, and hundreds of Jewish prisoners building the earthen ramp to access the wall. Ruthlessly deploying their catapults, the soldiers may have scaled the ramp under the cover of arrows and assailing boulders, leading the helpless Jewish rebels inside to make their terrible decision. ❖ The dry desert landscape was best executed with a sepia crayon on hot-pressed paper. Blending this with a tortillon produced a smooth effect, accentuating the light and shade, especially of those gigantic catapult boulders. I used an electric eraser to create the effect of a grainy terrain.

Off the Beaten Path: Goliaths of the Desert

Watercolor, 11 x 14

From a distance, these structures seemed to be made up of tiny bricks. Upon closer inspection, I realized that each of those "tiny" bricks was really a gigantic stone about six feet square and weighing more than three tons! I was completely overawed by their mammoth size. ❖ Fayez, my guide, told me that over two-and-a-half-million limestone blocks were deployed in the construction of the Great Pyramid alone. More than one hundred thousand workers toiled for over twenty years under the supervision of masons and architects. The blocks had to be placed very precisely to prevent pressure from the top resulting in the collapse of the whole structure. ❖ It was searing hot that late morning as we approached this incredible vista. My crafty guide had slipped past the long lines of tourists by taking a circuitous route through the desert, and I felt lucky to be afforded a view that was off the beaten path. ❖ Unfortunately, it became clear that Fayez had no interest in or patience for the work I was doing. "Wait cost extra pounds" was his consistent response any time I asked to stop so I might do a quick sketch or snap a few pictures. I acquiesced selectively, resigned to mentally adding pounds to my camel-ride meter. ❖ No matter the cost, however, this was a sight I didn't want to miss capturing through art. I made a watercolor pencil sketch and colored it in using my bottled water and a sable-hair brush. Using some photos to help me remember the details, I later created this piece on 400-pound cold-pressed paper, using dry-brush washes to capture the texture of stone and sand.

CHAPTER NINE

EGYPT ❖ GIZA

ETERNITY IN THE SANDS

Perched upon my camel somewhere in the sands of the Libyan Sahara, I was lost to the world.

It was hard to imagine that the Nile once flowed through a verdant landscape on this very spot, carrying barges laden with gigantic stones. At a pier now long gone, a royal procession would have disembarked along with somber priests robed in leopard-skin pelts muttering prayers from a sacred text. A wide causeway would have led the entourage to a city dotted with gleaming pyramids, pulsing with life. Architects and stonemasons worked with astronomers and countless workers using unimaginable contraptions to create these monumental structures that would long defy the elements. Through such a stone colossus, the god-king could reach out to the sun, basking in its eternally resplendent rays, so that he, the mighty pharaoh, could continue to live after he died.

There were no priests or incantations that morning, no pharaohs or ritual ceremonies. I couldn't hear the splash of the Nile ibises or the working sounds of farmers in the fields. Long gone was the chatter of builders and mathematicians busy with their measuring tools. There were no palaces or temples, no sight of those barges that would transport the god-king to the sun-god in the skies.

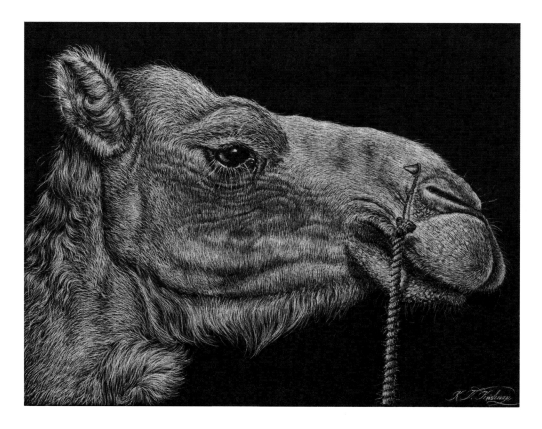

Camel Catastrophe: Resting from the Ride

Scratchboard, 9 x 12

I haven't had much luck with camels. I base this remark on my camel catastrophe in the Giza. ❖ Laden with cameras and film, I agreed to this "exotic, rarely conducted camel tour around the pyramids." Of course, I figured out much later that the tour was indeed "around" the pyramids because my guide did not want to pay the entrance fee to the Giza complex. ❖ So there I was in the midst of the Libyan Sahara, far from both monuments and humanity. My camel snorted loudly, at the behest of her master. Perched precariously upon her wobbly hump, towering at what seemed like fifty feet off the ground, I looked helplessly down at my guide. Gesticulating wildly, he was heatedly haggling with me, threatening to walk the camel — with me on top — further into the desert, should I not agree to his "new rate." ❖ "Fifty pounds extra," he persisted, lowering his bid. Previously I had stuck to a stubborn forty, but now, out of unashamed fear, I capitulated. ❖ Much later, I disembarked with relief. I took a final look at the beast, now absolutely nonchalant, who stood relaxed in the blazing sun. Her demeanor was so comically calm, given the threatening transaction that had earlier taken place, that I had to take some pictures. ❖ A few weeks later, in the air-conditioned comfort of my apartment, I used a scalpel to evoke the woolly fluff of her face and neck. Scratchboard was the inevitable medium to convey these distinctive textures.

In the distance, however, I could make out the shapes of those hallowed colossi that time had forgotten to sweep away. There were many more structures at one time than those that remain standing today. Still, these enormous structures, the pyramids, are one of the Seven Wonders of the Ancient World.

It was mid-morning, and an unending expanse of sculpted dunes basked in the harsh desert sun. Far away a camel caravan trundled in the sands of the Sahara. Countless travelers from exotic lands trudged along this very route eons ago, but their journeys took them into a prosperous city with palm trees, people, and shiny pyramids sheathed in polished limestone topped with pyramidions of gleaming gold.

I traveled with my family to timeless Giza, about six miles south of Cairo and at the edge of the Libyan Sahara. I hired a taxi at our Cairo hotel, and Mustafa, my driver, seemed to think that the awe-inspiring Great Pyramids of the Giza were a secret known only to the gods.

The Giza Plateau was part of the ancient capital of Memphis, from where the pharaohs ruled their lands. From my rocky outcrop, I could make out the shapes of the three famed pyramids — Khufu, Khafre, and Menkaure — guarded by the Great Sphinx (pages 162). It was an experience remarkably different from viewing photographs of these structures on the internet or in the guidebooks I lugged with me.

I was transported to a different world: a time of god-kings who planned their eternal lives through these indestructible monuments. When a pharaoh's earthly life came to an end, his mummified body was taken in a barge on the Nile to the location of the pyramid. Days of sacred chanting culminated in a somber procession that took the pharaoh's body to his final resting place. Walking in line were priests, mourners, and a retinue of slaves who bore all the paraphernalia the king would need for his next journey. His visceral organs were enshrined in hallowed canopic jars. Other treasures were placed in antechambers for him to use in his afterlife, including a grand barge of massive proportions. The pharaoh would then begin his procession towards the trail of the resplendent sun, walking in the footsteps of Ra, the mystic sun-god.

But the dead king, now alive in his afterlife, would need to speak. In the ritual called the Opening of the Mouth ceremony, the head priest, clad in a leopard pelt, would use a blade to touch the lips painted on the coffin, muttering magic spells as he did so. Now

deified as Horus, the falcon-headed god, the pharaoh would rejoice in the company of the brilliant sun in the mornings and wend his way to the land of Osiris as the orb sank into the evening skies.

Fayez seemed like a friendlier guide than the sullen Mustafa. He promised me an unforgettable tour around the pyramids and introduced me to his camel, Houri, the Beauty of the Sands. This albino dromedary — whose unusual feature, I later learned, resulted in additional charges against my wallet — grudgingly bent down to let me clamber up onto her back.

A Colossal Pair: The Great Sphinx and the Great Pyramid

Scratchboard, 16 x 20

Pondering this rather odd-looking giant in the sands, my guide reminded me that the Great Sphinx has had its face changed many times. Once it had even sported a beard, pieces of which were found between the Sphinx's paws by an archaeologist on a dig. Interestingly, my guide added that the word "sphinx" was a misnomer because the name derives from Greek mythology: Sphinx was the mythical winged beast with a woman's head and a lion's body that posed a riddle to the Thebans and killed all who couldn't answer. When an ancient historian visited Egypt, he thought it looked like the Greek Sphinx, and the name stuck. ❖ Enigmas and stories connected with the Great Sphinx are numerous. A book I purchased at a nearby stall dated the origin of the Sphinx to more than twelve thousand years ago. One story places the lost city of Atlantis somewhere under the Sphinx's paws! Another, positing that a tunnel stretched from the Sphinx to the Great Pyramids, has been discounted, although some subterranean passages were recently discovered underneath the figure. ❖ I moved between its paws, reliving the dream of King Thutmose IV. As a prince, he had once been out on a hunt and lay exhausted between the Sphinx's feet. He slept, and the Sphinx appeared to him in a dream, promising him the throne if he would clear the sand that had enveloped much of the stone figure. The prince agreed. ❖ From my vantage point, the Great Pyramid loomed behind the Sphinx. As if on cue, the sun broke away from a cloud bank, slanting down upon the silent colossus. A guide was clambering up the steps to point out something to his captive audience below. ❖ Scratchboard best captured the rough-hewn texture of stone, and I completed my work much later over a summer weekend in Tel Aviv.

SENTINELS OF THE SANDS

We approached the site from the cemetery complex lined with tombs of lesser queens and noblemen. In the slow gait of my ride, we passed several mastabas, smaller limestone and mud-brick tombs of ministers and queens. From where I was perched, I could see a vista of over nine pyramids splayed in the desert landscape: the famous trio, three queens' pyramids, and three smaller structures.

The pyramid of Pharaoh Khufu, from the twentieth-fifth century B.C.E., is the largest of the three principal structures on the Giza Plateau. It towers as the tallest pyramid in

Whatever Does It Say?: The Tomb of Ptahhotep

Pen and sepia wash, 11 x 14

Somewhere in the open-air ruins of Memphis, I stumbled upon the twin-tomb structure of father and son, Ptahhotep and Akhethotep, both wise viziers of the twenty-fifth century B.C.E. royal courts. The father, a well-respected historian, was noted for his thesis on social etiquette, presumably for misguided youth of those times. ❖ Entering the tomb, I was struck by the intricate carvings, reliefs, and hieroglyphs, all chockfull of scenes from daily life — the most well-preserved I had come across during my trip to Egypt. The splash of vegetable dyes brought out the life in human expressions, adding a sense of vividness to the scenes. These could have been painted twenty years ago, and I wouldn't have been able to tell the difference. ❖ In the frieze, children played upon a wall; a man, perhaps after a long day working, sipped wine from a cup; hunters were on the move looking for quarry; waterfowl and fish were being trapped in nets. ❖ In forty-five minutes that went by quickly, I had taken in a vast amount of Egyptian history, narrated in story on stone. Then I stepped outside onto the courtyard for fresh air. ❖ High above in one sunny nook I noticed a lintel with hieroglyphs. I didn't know what it meant to say, but the symbols were carved so uniformly they stood out boldly on the stone block. I couldn't help but wonder what people from long ago might have understood from the message upon this bright block of stone. ❖ I sketched it in pencil, later washing it with a couple of coats of India ink.

the world. Aptly known as the Great Pyramid, it rises majestically over 455 feet from the golden sands. Alas, the original smooth veneer of fine limestone was broken off over the centuries to be used for building mosques and the many ramparts of Cairo.

"It is more than forty stories tall," Fayez told me, pointing at the gigantic stone monument. "It was the tallest man-made structure in the world until the Eiffel Tower was erected in the 1800s."

The nearby pyramid of Khufu's son, the Pharaoh Khafre, is shorter by a few feet, but to me it seemed deceptively larger given its elevated position upon the sandy plain. This was the only pyramid that has retained a small cap of its original limestone cover, reminding me that centuries ago these colossi, coated with spotless white limestone, must have gleamed in the sun. A short camel ride away stood the pyramid dedicated to Khafre's son, the Pharaoh Menkaure. Nearby stood several smaller pyramids dedicated to his queens or daughters — no one knows for sure.

"Most pyramids had mystic symbols painted on their sides," Fayez said, and then went on to recount vivid descriptions by the Greek historian Herodotus, who had visited these lands in the fifth century B.C.E.

I had read about the mysteries of the Great Pyramid. Like the other eighty or so pyramids that have been excavated, the Pyramid of Khufu had an entrance that faced north towards the Pole Star. The burial chamber, however, faced west, towards the gloomy Kingdom of the Dead. And the mortuary temple faced east, towards the brilliance of the rising sun. Interestingly, no one has ever found a mummy inside the pyramid's cavernous vault.

From a distance, a climb to the top of the Pyramid of Khufu seemed tempting. As I approached it, though, the prospect seemed less inviting. A quick scramble led me to the present-day entrance, just below the original one. This led to a narrow corridor that ascended to the Grand Gallery.

It was an eerie feeling walking into more than forty-five hundred years of history. Crouching, I made my way along a narrow passageway, then huffed and puffed up a claustrophobic climb of some 130 feet, ending up in a small clearing. It was an Egyptian holiday, and I realized I was getting nudged from behind by restless teenagers who wanted me to move faster. Gasping for breath after an even steeper climb along the

Memento Moment: Djoser's Step Pyramid, Saqqara

Watercolor, 11 x 14

Built roughly thirty thousand years ago, the Step Pyramid is the oldest standing tomb on the planet. At two hundred feet high, it was designed for King Djoser of the Third Dynasty by his vizier, Imhotep. Here, the brilliant courtier constructed something remarkable for his King in the afterlife: several mastabas (rectangular structures with sloping sides and a flat roof) stacked in elegant artistry, soaring up to the endless blue sky. ❖ There was no shade to rest in, so I merely dismounted my dromedary perch and took a few pictures. A month later I painted the scene on a sheet of 400-pound cold-pressed paper. For better or worse, it will always remind me of an annoying incident that occurred there. ❖ Having watched me with my camera, a couple of enterprising peddlers descended upon me. I allowed them to whisk me to a nearby tent that housed an array of Egyptian statuettes made, they assured me, of the heaviest stone available. An ardent fan of anything having to do with art, I conceded to temptation and traded a whole lot of Egyptian pounds for what I felt was one of their choicest souvenir sphinxes. ❖ Later, I arrived at the Chicago airport with my prize in tow. The joyless customs official glared. "Is that a mummy?" he snapped. Muttering under my breath, I began unraveling my heavy parcel, tenderly swathed in bandages, as a curious audience of fellow passengers waited behind in line. I was greatly relieved when I got grudging permission to proceed. ❖ A year later, a visiting friend eyed my sphinx. "Where did you get it?" he asked. After I told him, he remarked, "I bought an identical one just last week at my local department store." ❖ Of course I had to immediately surf the Web, only to find several listings from online sites that bring such items right to your doorstep. And what's worse, for a fifty percent discount and shipping and handling thrown in for free!

Grand Gallery, I stood gazing in wonder at the narrow room with its stone sarcophagus. Curiously, the sarcophagus seemed much wider than the narrow passageway through which it could have been brought inside.

I later visited the adjacent Solar Boat Museum. As is the case with many other pyramids, several barges were buried in nearby pits to enable the pharaoh to sail along the Nile to meet the gods. This building housed an entire boat nearly five thousand years old; some of the oars reaching thirty feet long were still intact. As was typical for the time, the

planks had been lashed together using ropes made simply of vegetable fiber.

Past the Valley Temple crouched the enigmatic Great Sphinx (pages 154-5). With a lion's body and a human face, this sentinel-divinity of Giza provided a comforting contrast to the severe geometry of the pyramids. This gigantic recumbent figure, with its paws extended, stretched 240 feet in length and more than sixty feet in height. Carved out of a natural outcrop of rock around the time of the construction of the pyramid of Khafre, the Great Sphinx may have been shaped to resemble the sun-god, or even Khafre himself.

A Forgotten Capital

The next day, I was back in the Sahara, once again tenaciously holding onto my camel mount. I had taken a taxi from Cairo to the ancient kingdom of Memphis. Founded by the legendary Pharaoh Menes in 3100 B.C.E., the city rose to glory by becoming the first capital of the united Upper and Lower Egypt, prospering for over four hundred years. One of the most populous cities of the world, the place once teemed with palaces and gardens. Sadly, all that remained were tenements where the poorest residents lived and a small museum with broken statues from the temples around the complex.

There It Is!: Step Pyramid from the Valley Temple of Unas, Saqqara

Acrylic on canvas board, 11 x 14

Rather than drive from Memphis, I approached Saqqara on camelback along this cruel stretch of the Sahara. I neared the Valley Temple of Unas that lay in the quiet of the sands. Recently reconstructed, a long causeway connected this temple to the mortuary shrine and the Pyramid of Unas, which is but a heap of rubble today. ❖ Suddenly, Saqqara's most famous site —the majestic Step Pyramid— appeared on the horizon projecting out from the dunes. It was a surreal afternoon; the sun was out, but a sandstorm seemed to be brewing. The blue skies darkened and a dusty brown haze covered the horizon, lending a sense of intrigue to the vista. ❖ There were a few restored columns around the temple, but a couple of palm trees farther from the foreground caught my eye. At that moment, I noticed a camel rider coming in for a closer look. He surveyed the scene from upon an outcrop, and I was very taken with the triangular composition created by the pyramid, the palm tree, and the rider. ❖ Avoiding eye contact with my jockey of the day lest he start grumbling about money, I proceeded to sketch the scene. In twenty minutes, I made a watercolor draft. Unfortunately, a couple of my sketches from earlier in the morning decamped in the brisk winds; chasing after them among the dunes would have been futile. ❖ Months later, I recreated this landscape in acrylic on a canvas board. A hog-hair fan brush did wonders, allowing me to render the sky into pointillist mottles and add texture to muddy sand and stone.

When Memphis was the glorious capital of Egypt during the Old Kingdom, nearby Saqqara was its necropolis. It was here that the brilliant vizier Imhotep, disregarding all architectural conventions, created the first gigantic Step Pyramid for King Djoser (pages 167 and 168). Deceased pharaohs, family members, and sacred animals were ceremoniously brought to Saqqara from Memphis to be permanently enshrined within its mortuary sanctums. Here, they would lie in the silence of the centuries to come.

It was evening, and I had driven back to Giza with my family. The pyramids were silhouetted in the resplendence of the setting sun, appearing just as the pharaohs would have wanted them to look in their repose: kissed by the beams of Amun-Ra, that brilliant divinity of the skies. It was easy to transport myself to those times when a golden pyramidion capstone would have gleamed in the sun, and pilgrims from near and far would have come to pay homage to the dead king who continued to shower prosperity on them in his afterlife.

Secrets of the Stones

Connecting the land with the skies, these tall monuments let kings of yore commune with their gods in heaven. But were these marvels in stone mere burial monuments, or did they house mysteries far beyond the comprehension of the empirical mind?

It was hard for me to separate what scientists contend to be mystical mumbo-jumbo from the technical genius of the ancient Egyptians. However, I also had a hard time casually dismissing some unexplained facts. For one, to date no one really has figured out how the pyramids were constructed. Three or four building methods have been offered as possibilities, but they are merely speculations.

"These pyramids could have been observatories," a research scholar I met at the Cairo Museum told me. Ancient Egyptians were obsessed with astronomy and the stars. From Strabo to Newton to other scientists over the years, there have been theories posited as to how accurately aligned these pyramids are with the cardinal points, the meridians, Polaris, and certain constellations. Several narrow tunnels that seemingly serve no purpose crisscross inside the pyramids.

Another presenter explained that it was quite likely that the pharaohs had these structures built in their lifetimes so they could get initiated into the secret lore of death and afterlife even when they were alive, thereby preparing them for a supreme life eternal.

An ancient proverb reads: Everything fears Time — but Time fears the Pyramids. ❖

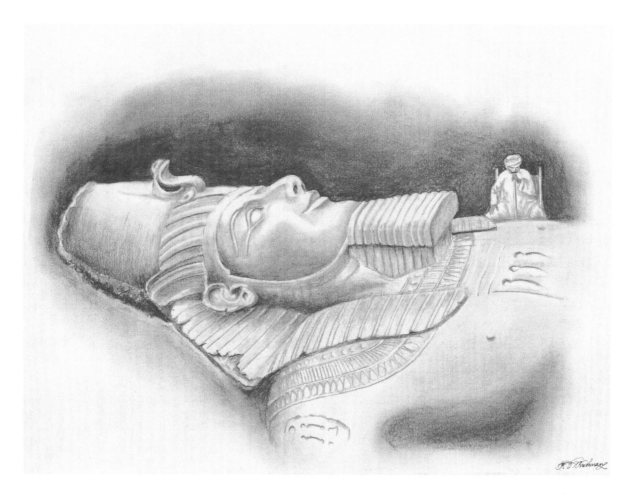

Sleepy Sentinel: Memphis

Conté crayon, 11 x 14

I walked around the open-air museum that comprises what's left of Memphis today and ended up in an enclosure. I gasped at the sheer size of the fallen forty-foot limestone statue of Rameses II. In ancient times, perhaps, it had stood in a courtyard, greeting pilgrims to the Great Temple of Ptah. ❖ I clambered up to a balcony that let me view this scene from above. ❖ The mystery of the now legless sculpture lies not in the enormity of the figure but in its sheer perfection. The details that were achieved by master craftsmen are breathtaking. The belt, the dagger, the bracelets are all so delicately carved on a stone that is less than stable! I moved around trying to take in the prone figure in its entirety but couldn't find a suitable vantage point in that small two-story shelter. ❖ In despair I got down to ground level and took some pictures. Later, back in my hotel room, I sketched a crayon drawing, adding in the details and smudging the color with my fingers. ❖ I didn't want to leave out the guard, who, unmindful of my existence, rested his chin on his stick and slept though the entire exercise as if posing for this picture!

Inside the Serapeum:
The Catacomb of the Sacred Bulls

India ink and brush, 11 x 14

The Great Temple of Ptah was once the city's most prominent structure, dedicated to the creator god who had simply "thought" the world into existence. In Memphis, this deity was worshipped by the cult of the Apis bull. ❖ Enclosed within the temple grounds, a chosen bull was accorded all the respect and adulation a god deserved. The priests maintained that its mother must have been struck by a bolt of lightning that caused her to conceive a handsome calf with a diamond patch on its forehead, two white hairs on its tail, and the shape of an eagle on its back. When this sacred animal died, it was mummified and carried ceremoniously in a procession to be entombed in Saqqara. ❖ The bull was a link between the pharaoh and the creator god, connecting the living divinity on earth to the one in the heavens. ❖ The Serapeum was deserted that sunny afternoon as I walked through its pitch-dark portals. I could well imagine masked priests leading the procession, with the mummified bull hoisted upon an alabaster slab. ❖ In a dank chamber, I came upon this enormous sarcophagus with its lid partly open. The ancient devout would have lined up here as they waited their turn to salute their bovine divinity, wishing it well on its mystical quest. ❖ I took a photograph and later painted this in five coats of India ink. Black and white best captured the paleness of death, the dimness of the subterranean catacombs, and the spotlight cast on the massive sarcophagus by a flickering light bulb. In this ghostly milieu, a lone guard suspiciously watched my movements from upon a stone ledge, adding a sense of scale to the scene.

Hunting for a Shark:
Sunset at Giza

Watercolor, 12 x 16

Tired but recharged on our second evening in the Giza desert, I ended up — unbelievably enough — at a Pizza Hut with a commanding view of the Great Sphinx and the Pyramids. ❖ However, there was a stir in the family — Anish, then five, had just realized that he'd left his beloved toy shark somewhere in the desert. Hysterically, he demanded that we retrace our steps all the way to Giza, Memphis, and Saqqara so we could find his aquatic friend. Several bargains were proposed, but to no avail. ❖ In the middle of this melee, I noticed the sun going down. Perhaps selfishly, I left the family inside the Pizza Hut and dashed out with my camera to take in the view of the sun between those two great monuments. The third pyramid seemed to blaze with fire caught from the brilliantly lit skies. The Khafre and Khufu pyramids loomed large, their silhouettes taking up most of the foreground. ❖ A hot, hurrying breeze was sweeping the dusty, sandy ground into a frenzy, sending billowing clouds up the pyramids. I could barely make out the clutter of humanity in the foreground, but I could see a lone camel rider to my left who had, like me, paused to take in this sight. ❖ I took a few photographs, but made a conscious effort to capture nature's palette in my mind. Even today, I still vividly recall the red, violet and gold colors as well as a dominant sunbeam striking at a cloud bank. ❖ All this needed to be expressed in art — as a tribute to the brilliant Amun-Ra clad in his raiment of the setting sun. I used 400-pound cold-pressed paper, layering ten washes to reproduce the translucency of the skies. ❖ Even then I knew it was the best souvenir I could take back with me. Yes, and the next morning I did find another toy shark at the Cairo airport to replace its missing brother, although as my son pointed out, it was much smaller and less friendly-looking.

The Legend of the Oracle

Scratchboard, 18 x 14

According to ancient Greek mythology, our planet is shaped like a flat disc. Zeus, god of gods, wanting to find the center of the earth, dispatched two vultures to reconnoiter from the skies. These birds ascended upon Mount Parnassus, having spotted the omphalos near the sanctuary of Apollo in Delphi. ❖ My guide, Nikos, and I looked long at the ruins before us. In the silence, it was hard to imagine that here once thronged the devout theopropoi from faraway lands. My guide remarked that at the height of its glory, the number of oracles increased to three to serve the many pilgrims who came from all the Greek islands as well as from the faraway dominions of the Black Sea and what's now called Spain. ❖ Scratchboard seemed to be the best medium to capture the crags of the mountains as a backdrop to the theatrical setting of the Temple of Apollo. ❖ I made a few sketches and took several photographs for the detail, later completing my work over three weeks in my apartment in downtown Athens.

CHAPTER TEN

GREECE ❖ DELPHI

THE LEGEND OF THE ORACLE

Below the loom of Mount Parnassus, I stood gazing at the quiet sprawl of ruins that long ago was the Temple of Apollo. A seemingly endless swath of olive groves stood in the distance. Here, long ago, the oracle ruled supreme, famed across centuries of power for her stunningly accurate predictions.

Apollo, it was believed, always spoke through a chaste priestess who presented a curiously fearsome sight. Seated upon a tripod and chewing laurel leaves, the wizened woman muttered and convulsed, inhaling mystic fumes emerging through a mysterious fissure in the earth. The attendant priests always found a way to make perfect sense of her incoherent utterances, conveying these portentous predictions in iambic verse.

The theopropoi, pilgrims from faraway lands, bowed down reverentially, satisfied with the outpourings they would cherish as they trudged back to their distant homelands.

This awe-inspiring scene would have been a common one two thousand years ago. Here among the ruins of the Temple of Apollo in Delphi (left and pages 185-6), three hours from crowded Athens, I was standing where once sat the Pythian oracle, making her predictions over the centuries with eerie accuracy.

Looming ahead of me were the cruel crags of Mount Parnassus where the mythical Muses lived and many a Greek play was staged. I shuddered to think that it was

from one of these peaks that the Delphians had hurled Aesop the storyteller to his death for having mocked the citizens of the city. Not far from this lush green landscape, Oedipus — of Freudian fame — unwittingly slew his father, King Laius. To my right was graceful Mount Kirphys, clothed in an unending expanse of olive trees, disappearing into the vast plains below and embracing the waters of the Bay of Itea. From where I was taking in this scene, I could make out the old Delphic theater and the rubble of treasuries, statues, and columns where once had thrived a great civilization.

Shaky Start: Ionic Column

Whiteboard and ink, 11 x 14

I boarded the bus from Athens to Delphi right after the cab driver ripped me off. He had picked me up from Nikodimou Street where I stayed and dropped me off at the bus stand, but only after taking the most circuitous route to that point, with a couple of unnecessary city sights thrown in. ❖ The previous evening I had endured a highly unpleasant experience. Athens seems to have a well-organized mafia supervising the operation of everything from souvenir stands to popcorn kiosks. I had drifted into a pub and ran up a tab of 10,000 drachmas ($40 USD) for two glasses of pineapple juice and a bowl of stale cashew nuts. The "manager" soon showed up, complaining that since my credit card was not approved, I needed to go to the nearest bank to withdraw drachmas. Escorted by a burly, menacing fellow, I drove off to the nearest ATM. Shaken, I got the money and paid up. Afterwards, I swore to myself never to prowl the nighttime streets of Athens again. (Later, when I received my monthly card statement, I noticed my card had indeed been swiped, but for 63,000 drachmas, or $250 USD, in an institution called Plato's Paradise.) ❖ However, these episodes did not significantly detract from my Delphi experience — something I vowed to enjoy with a vengeance. Walking along the Sacred Way not far from the Temple of Apollo, I came upon this lone Ionic column. I was fascinated by the contrast of the scene: the lush green groves, the sad array of broken stones, and the velvety purple of the distant mountains against the harsh crags of Mount Parnassus. In this setting, the fluted column gleamed against the morning sun, revealing its intricate carvings made by dexterous hands more than two thousand years ago. ❖ I took a few photos and made a few sketches. I used a whiteboard and colored in the scene with ink, scratching in the details with a stylus. This seemed to be the best medium to capture the spirit of the moment.

It wasn't just this vision of a mystic spokeswoman of the gods, or the spectacularly scenic backdrop, or the recalling of ancient Greek legends that gave this place a sense of sanctity. For here was located the hallowed omphalos, the navel of the earth, and the very center of the universe of the ancient Greeks.

Nikos, my Greek guide, drew for me the famous isosceles triangle of sacred places: Delphi equidistantly triangulating the Acropolis in Athens and the Temple of Olympia. "Other theories," he added in evident disbelief, "suggest an even larger isosceles triangle, connecting Delphi to points as far away as the navel centers in Africa and Asia."

Rain Drenched and Light Washed:
Verdant Olive Groves

Watercolor, 11 x 14

Kalamata olives are one of the most common products in any Greek supermarket in the United States, and I have always wondered why Greece and olives are so intertwined. Though the city of Kalamata is located in southern Greece, in Athens, to the northwest, olives were a prominent feature (along with, incidentally, cats!) during both my stay and my visits to many of the tourist spots in the area. ❖ *Walking along the Via Sacra, not far from the numerous treasuries scattered all along the way to the Temple of Apollo, I chanced upon this spectacular scene. The loom of harsh Mount Parnassus nurtured the millions of olive trees that stretched a verdant blanket upon the valley of Phocis as far as the eye could see. Far beyond me, I could make out the glimmer of the Bay of Itea and its waters that led to the Corinthian Gulf.* ❖ *For a few seconds, gray clouds crowded together in the skies in an attempt to veil the sun that cleaved through rain, clothing the distant mountains in burnished gold. Below me, a path snaked into the distance past the mountain cliffs, losing itself in the green carpet. I enjoyed a brief rain shower, and when that stopped, I whipped out my sketchpad, making quick notes of the strange interplay of light and shade in the canvas of the skies.* ❖ *I painted this scene in watercolor on heavy cold-pressed paper, dragging my dry brush to capture the effect of the olive groves. I used masking fluid and a blade to highlight the speckle of sunlight upon rock and applied several washes to capture the unique experience of the moment.* ❖ *Oddly enough, even before I was done, a cat came up to me, meowing, and decided to use my jeans as a scratching post. Such was the mellow mood I was in that it received only a gentle rub in return!*

A CULT OF YORE

It was a sunny April morning when I waited for a bus in the Odos Liosion Street station. After a scenic three-hour ride from the plains of the city and its suburbs into mountainous terrain, the bus unloaded its human fare into the quiet main street of Delphi. Very quickly, the new gave way to the old as the silent columns of the Agora, the marketplace of those times, came into view.

"The name *Delphi* originates from the hero *Delphos*, son of Apollo and a nymph, Kastelia," Nikos said, "who was immortalized by the spring that bears her name."

I learned that this town had been an oracular center since the fourteenth century B.C.E., during which time it was believed that Gaia, the goddess of the earth, was making her predictions through her son, Python. According to legend, the infant Apollo sought out the fearsome Python and killed him, exacting an old revenge. Later, having become worthy of worship in this sacred land, Apollo gave his oracular predictions through the Pythia — women over fifty who had led a life of unsullied purity. The god gave his prophesies while residing in the shrine for nine months. During the other three, he would visit people in the icy Nordic lands far to the north.

In commemoration of Apollo's victory over Python, the Pythian Games were instituted in 582 B.C.E., with a gala celebration and sports. Years of earthquakes, pillaging rulers, and the rise of other cults did not deter Delphi's popularity. Many wars were fought for conquest and defense of this cultic township. Over the centuries, the sanctuary was maintained by an overflowing treasury filled with offerings from kings and peasants alike who consulted the oracle.

The Romans conquered the city in the second century B.C.E. The ruthless emperor Nero once pillaged the shrine and decamped with over five hundred statues from the shrine of Apollo. The cult at Delphi still survived for another four hundred years, but its fame started waning.

"Apollo has no cell, the fair-wrought hall has fallen . . ." had once uttered the oracle, in a prophetic utterance when Julian the Apostate, the last emperor of Rome, consulted the Pythia. The shrine was finally closed in 381 C.E. by the Christian emperor Theodosius who set about decimating anything that smacked of paganism.

An Interrupted Bargain: Treasury of the Athenians

Acrylic, 14 x 18

A bargain, the wag says, is struck when two people are sure they each got the better of the other. In parts of Southeast Asia, the calculator can be an effective way to bridge the linguistic gap. Bargains struck in Europe's flea markets generally require less vigorous interaction. Here in Greece, there's still the periodic fist-thumping and chest-beating. It is only when one wanders further westward that subtle body language takes over from wild gesticulations and well-staged theatrics. ❖ A peddler caught my eye along the Sacred Way. He tried to sell me a pen-sized Ionic column, with a Doric one thrown in for good measure. As I threw myself into a lively round of haggling, Nikos, who was now adept in gauging my interest in all memento moments and impressionist ones, tapped me on the shoulder. ❖ A beautiful sight greeted my eyes. The sun was slanting down that cloudy morning, setting the mountains afire. In front of me stood the Treasury of the Athenians, where citizens of the city would deposit their offerings to the oracle in return for her farsighted predictions. A tithe of one-tenth of one's earnings was common back then. The Rock of Sibyl, a weather-worn, mossy boulder from which an oracle in the days of Gaia gave her predictions, was just ahead of me to the right. It seemed a very apt setting, and I admired how the barren treasure troves now glistened with gold of a different kind. ❖ I made several mental notes and recreated this scene from memory several weeks later. ❖ Unfortunately, I couldn't consummate that two for one bargain, as another unsuspecting tourist had engaged the vendor's attention.

Shadow of a Shrine: Pillars of the Temple of Apollo

Conté crayon, 11 x 14

The thing I have found with guides is that it can be hard to separate fact from fable. With his palpable enthusiasm for anything and everything Greek, my guide, Nikos, had a captive audience in me for over eight hours. ❖ While I used a sepia Conté crayon to sketch this scene at the shrine, he kept me entertained with a thirty-minute narrative on the Temple of Apollo, its history, legends, old wives' tales, and more; it was just enough time to finish my picture. ❖ Mythology tells us that the first shrine was made of laurel leaves, the second of beeswax and feathers, the third of bronze provided by the goddess Athena and the fourth was made by a couple of mythical architects with the help of Apollo. ❖ However, from a point of historical fact, Nikos said, these ruins date from the third temple of Apollo. The first structure, built in 650 B.C.E., was made of porous stone and was destroyed by fire. It was replaced by a building built by an Athenian clan; it was completely devastated by a massive earthquake in 373 B.C.E. ❖ Donations flowed in from various parts of the world, even from nations as far away as Egypt, and a new shrine was built upon the same spot where its predecessors had stood. This was finished in 330 B.C.E. It must have indeed been a handsome structure in the days of yore, when Delphi was a seat of oracular power.

Rebus Revenge: The Sphinx of Naxos

Conté crayon on cream pastel paper, 14 x 11

The museum displayed the works of art excavated at Delphi by the French School. I eventually came up to the Hall of the Charioteer, which houses the most popular sculpture in the museum. Carved in the fifth century B.C.E., this sculpture of a jockey was a piece from a larger one depicting a quadriga — a four-horse chariot deployed in the games of the time. ❖ A little later on, the beautiful marble figurine of this sphinx caught my eye. Until Nikos cracked the code for me, I didn't know that the word "sphynx" in Greek means "strangler" — nemesis of the hapless who can't figure out the rebus. ❖ Differing from its Egyptian counterpart, there was a gender change: this mythical creature had the head of a woman, the front of a bird, the body of a lion, and the tail of a snake. It sat atop a thirty-five-foot column facing the forbidden sanctum of Apollo's shrine from where the oracle prophesied. Now mounted on a short column, it was a gift from the people of the island of Naxos to Delphi in 560 B.C.E. (Months later, I did notice a less stylish, white replica when I visited the port of Naxos on one of those ubiquitous Greek Island tours.) ❖ A German tourist who had flown in from Munich for a long weekend found my quick sketch very intriguing. Helmut was so fascinated by Greek history that he had majored in that subject and was teaching it at a local school in Hamburg. ❖ It took me less than twenty minutes to sketch this in crayon. In my Athens apartment the next day, I smoothed the texture using a simple blending stump I fashioned out of tightly rolled paper.

NESTLED IN NATURE

Interestingly, the town seemed remarkably casual given the history that gave it such fame. There were no signs directing visitors to the sanctuary or to the museum, nor to the nearby ruins of Athena Pronaia, which nestled in the niches of the mountains. As I walked along the scenic highway towards ancient Arahova, I noticed the forest of olive trees blanketing the slopes of the mountains around me. I could imagine anxious pilgrims landing on these very shores, their offerings in hand, wondering how their futures would be revealed to them in the coming hour.

In less than quarter of a mile I was walking along the Via Sacra, the Sacred Way, the way of the ancient pilgrim. The style of monuments around the public square, known as the Agora, was typically Roman, after the many emperors who had both pillaged and restored the shrine. Long ago, these must have once glimmered with treasures from distant lands.

"Probably even the golden throne of Midas may have once been hidden in these crypts," my guide intoned.

Along the stony climb, hugged by the sweep of the theater, I came upon the majestic shrine of Apollo. It was within its mysterious precincts that the oracle had poured out her divine mutterings. Alas, only a few columns and some circular stone steps remain to remind us of its storied history.

The shrine was a Doric structure. It is recorded that in the portico had stood a statue of Homer, and words of pithy wisdom were inscribed on stone — Know thyself; Nothing in excess — along with a mysterious "E," which has not yet been infallibly interpreted. The Seven Sages and numerous philosophers from Plutarch to Pindar trod upon these very steps. Altars and statues may have adorned every nook and cranny.

A theater that splayed in front of me was built in the fourth century B.C.E. and held over five thousand spectators along rows of stone seats. It was within this enclosure that Greek tragicomedies were enacted in the past. A further short climb from here, and surrounded by conifer trees, lay what was once the stadium of Delphi, where skilled jockeys goaded their horses towards victory. I could imagine the sounds of the Pythian Games when hurrah after hurrah must have cheered on the quadrigas, speedy chariots of those times, in their finishing laps.

Plodding along the road to Arahova I came across a gymnasium that overlooked the shrine of Athena Pronaia, powerful protectress of the more famous shrine to her half-brother, Apollo. A landslide of gigantic rocks from Mount Parnassus, said to have been perpetrated by this goddess, had halted the incursion of the Persian army invading Delphi in the fifth century B.C.E. Even more remarkable, this miraculous incident was said to have been prophesied by the oracle long ago. The flummoxed Persians fled, never to return.

Nestled among these verdant olive trees was the enigmatic Doric shrine of

Tholos (pages 190-1). It was an elegant rotunda built of marble in the fourth century B.C. and probably served as a shrine of Gaia. "It's an unsurpassed architectural masterpiece of its kind," Nikos commented, adding that the design was intricately built around complex algebraic calculations, including ratios using the golden number.

Past a few more ruins and smaller treasuries in this complex, I had now retraced the path of the pious. In those days, weary but eager pilgrims from faraway lands would have disembarked near Itea and climbed the northern slopes of the Pleistos Valley towards the shrines in Marmaria. Having worshipped at the shrine of Athena Pronaia, they would then perform their ritual ablutions at the Castalian Spring, shopped for votive offerings near the Agora, and walked along the Sacred Way. Proceeding towards the holy precincts of the Apollo shrine, they would have deposited their offerings in the various treasuries along the way and then worshipped at the Temple of Apollo. Formalities completed, they could finally attend to the prophecies of the divine oracle.

AN EPIC SETTING

It was evening as I trudged back to the bus stand. Tenacious myrtle and lentisk shrubs struggled for a toehold in the sweep of the mountainside. The sun set fire to the stately rocks of Mount Parnassus wrought by centuries of winds, wars, and worship. Dark clouds and a crack of thunder warned me of the coming wrath of the mountain gods. Mother Nature's guardians, the goddess Gaia and her daughter Themis, seemed to speak to me through the rustle of the trees and the trickle of hidden water coursing among the rocks.

As the bus wended its way back to Athens, it wasn't hard to imagine how the legend of the oracle had once thrived in these picturesque mountains. For even in the tangle of modern buildings and contemporary roads, I could truly feel an intangible force in that age-old town — difficult to completely fathom through my earthly senses, but it was subtly, surely felt. ❖

Mathematical Mystery: Tholos

Watercolor, 14 x 18

Many artists curse cloudy days, but I love those intervals when the bashful sun decides to play hide-and-seek with me, letting me in on secrets that few tourists get to see and record. I walked more than half a mile from the Temple of Apollo to the shrines of Marmaria, and came upon what is probably one of the most enigmatic structures in Delphi. ❖ *There was nothing to break the silence — no birds, no tourists, not even the faintest sounds of a human presence. The sweep of greenery and stones in disarray made a perfect setting for this speckled marble monument that seemed to radiate serenity. It stood on three, tiered Doric legs and bore a curvy broken slab of marble on its head. No one really knows what the Tholos was constructed for, though a popular guidebook refers to this structure as an old temple dedicated to Gaia, the earth goddess, while another one claims it was a treasury where statues were once housed. Was its shape simply evocative of the omphalos, a kind of preview before pilgrims reached the sanctum of Apollo where the real stone was housed? It is a mystery.* ❖ *Built in the fourth century B.C.E. by one Theodorus from Asia Minor, the Tholos must have been a mathematical marvel — a circular structure with twenty Doric columns in the exterior circle and probably ten Corinthian columns in an inner one. Today, only three reconstructed outer columns stood — sentinels from a previous era.* ❖ *It was late morning as the sun broke though its shackle of clouds, spilling over mountaintops and dappling the ruins through the blanket of trees. A lone man with a stick wended his way towards the stone circle. I took several pictures and created this watercolor drawing on hot-pressed paper so I could render the details more thoroughly.*

Rapt Reptile: El Castillo on a Cloudy Day

Acrylic on paper, 12 x 16

The structure that stood before me was an astronomical wonder. The monument was made of 365 steps — in keeping with the number of days of an average year. Stairways divided the nine terraces on each side of the pyramid into eighteen segments, representing the eighteen months of the Maya calendar. ❖ *From an altar atop the pyramid, the priest would have whispered to a crowded courtyard of worshippers below, but the genius of acoustic design would have magnified his voice into a thunderous sermon.* ❖ *Across to my left was a throng of tourists headed to the Temple of Warriors. A mass of clouds loomed on the horizon that would have once made the Maya truly cheerful. A hazy light beamed down upon the pyramid from the sun that was struggling to emerge from the clouds. I was particularly struck by the sight of an iguana — a common denizen of these parts — who looked mesmerized by this scene.* ❖ *I hastily sketched all this using a stack of colored pencils. A couple of teenage vendors, who presumably lived in the village nearby, got very interested in what I was doing and even asked me to draw their portraits. I had to tell them that human subjects didn't come under the jurisdiction of my artistic expertise!* ❖ *I completed this painting in the quiet of my Chicago studio a few months later.*

CHAPTER ELEVEN

MEXICO ❖ CHICHEN ITZA

SLITHER OF THE PLUMED SERPENT

I had traveled back in time more than a thousand years to an equinox ritual in the great shrine of El Castillo. I could see it in my mind's eye: High above, the head priest stood upon the platform atop this stone pyramid. The Maya elite muttered spells as commoners jostled one another in the courtyard below. Warriors in fearsome attire lined up along the sacred causeways, and a deadly game of pok-ta-pok had just concluded in the Great Ball Court. Astronomers with their plumb bobs and crossed sticks made notes at the observatory of El Caracol. Sacrificial victims, painted blue, cowered on the steps, awaiting their inevitable fate.

At that magical moment caused by a dramatic interplay of light, shadow, and stone, the plumed snake-god Kukulcan descended from the Maya heavens, slithering down the stone stairway to the ground below, banishing drought and disease, showering the parched lands with rain and abundance.

I stood in the vast complex of Chichen Itza in the Yucatan Peninsula — a glorious remnant of an ancient Maya civilization.

Just that morning, I had left the lovely seaside resort of Cancun and a bus ride of two-and-a-half hours had brought me to this courtyard bristling with pyramids and thousand-year-old monuments that nestled in the sunny Mexican peninsula that juts out into the blue waters of the Caribbean.

This stretch of land houses the "old Chichen" area, which was occupied between the sixth and tenth centuries C.E., and the "new Chichen" site, which dates back to between the eleventh and thirteenth centuries. Their architectural themes contrasted sharply.

"There are several theories for this variation in architecture," my guide, Ariel explained. "The older Chichen style is influenced by buildings of the older Puuc Maya, whereas the newer Chichen Itza has monuments that depict bravery, aggression, and human sacrifice, possibly owing to the incursion in this region of the Itza tribe, who brought in Toltec influences from central Mexico."

Wide roads, called sacbes, connect the larger monuments, and it is believed that this network of byways represented the network of stars in the Milky Way.

For the ancient Maya, astronomy was everything.

A FLAME EXTINGUISHED

I read that the earliest Maya peoples inhabited the Yucatan peninsula for at least nine thousand years. Many of the later tribes may have lived here in thatched huts, leading an agricultural lifestyle. In the sixth century C.E., a group of Puuc Maya settled in the township of Chichen around a couple of sinkholes, known as cenotes, that offered access to groundwater.

Chichen soon began its rise to prominence with the arrival of seafaring Itza merchants in the ninth century. These traders settled by the larger cenote, giving the city its name: The City of the Wise Men of the Water. In those years, Chichen Itza must have been a great center of culture, trade, and ceremonial worship. On a darker note, this period also saw the celebration of human sacrifice as an honorable means by which to enter the realms of paradise.

Wars and strife shook the formerly tranquil community, and over the next several centuries it was pillaged and resettled many times. In the early fifteenth century, however, it was mysteriously abandoned. By the time the Spanish

Talking in Smiles: Kukulcan Balustrade

Conté crayon, 9 x 12

Kukulcan was revered as the feathered serpent-god whom the Aztecs called Quetzalcoatl. All around the Chichen Itza complex, three things struck me as being ubiquitous: Kukulcan, chac mools and lazy iguanas! ❖ As I walked about the Temple of Warriors, I came across this beautiful stone balustrade rendering the mysterious snake-god and a human standard-bearer above the serpent's head. During celebratory events a warrior would have held a colorful banner that fluttered in the wind. ❖ With interest I observed a few Maya pilgrims near me who were circling the sacred grounds of their forefathers. Much to their curiosity I began a simple crayon work, quickly drawing the outline of light and shade. We spoke in smiles, the most common language of footloose international "vagabonds" like me. ❖ The sun was smiling down in full blaze. It was 2 P.M., and the snake head stood out boldly against the surrounding stonescape, its teeth glinting. Later, a blending stump helped with the 3D effects. ❖ Afterwards, when mentioning this encounter to Ariel, he told me that while the Maya culture was dead, the race itself had survived. Some of the Maya managed to live through the conquests, though their native tongue was eventually displaced by Spanish influence. Being of Maya descent himself, he speculated, the bane of disease brought by the Spaniards had probably all but wiped out a race. ❖ But some believe, he added, that the Maya emigrated to the fabled Atlantis. ❖ This I couldn't buy, but it made a very imaginative story.

Death for Eternity: Pok-ta-pok Ball Court

Watercolor washes on paper, 9 x 12

My guide, Ariel, and I gazed at this ancient ball court. I couldn't help but mentally reenact the deadly game that was played in Mesoamerican cultures for over three thousand years. According to the sacred Maya text of Popul Vuh, the two opposing forces symbolized good versus evil, with the winning team embodying the good. A lot of ceremonious fanfare preceded the game, which was seen as an act of selfless worship to the gods. ❖ It was quite sunny as we strolled around the enormous court, staring at the carved hoop high over our heads, one each on opposite walls. I had a hard time imagining how even the most skillful player could deflect a ball up so high using only his hip. ❖ This was a ten-minute watercolor sketch. I used a dry brush as I tried to capture the texture of the stone, shadow, the bright sunlight and the blue skies in the background.

When is Lunch?: Iguana Basking on the Rocks

Scratchboard, 5 x 7

Crumbling stone walls surround the Tulum complex. Seeming to have been some sort of a protected city, it was clearly well defended by what would have been at that time a solid wall on three sides and the Caribbean Sea on the fourth. ❖ My wife, Ramaa, espied a lazy iguana basking in the sun, waiting, perhaps, for the drone of the stingless bee. A very obedient portrait model, it posed for me motionless, letting me pull out a scratchboard and use my line tool for over thirty minutes, etching out the details, before it made its next move — a mere few inches away before it began its next long wait for lunch! ❖ I felt I needed to color the brilliant blue skies, the turquoise waters, and a bit of those dense green thickets around me. Later, I painted this with waterproof ink over three layers of application.

Heart and Blood: Chac Mool Awaits

Scratchboard, 11 x 14

Sacrificial victims, rounded up from the ravages of war and conquest, would have watched the scene — some in horror and perhaps a few in muted reverence, confident that the immutable Maya paradise was probably just moments away. Maybe they glanced at the figure of this warrior, supported on its elbows and holding a bowl that would hold yet another sacrifice of blood and a beating heart. ❖ While the imagery was gory, the ambience around me was contrastingly serene. It was a moonlit night as I waited for the sound and light show to commence at Chichen Itza. The tourist groups hadn't descended upon this place yet. Far away from the rusty metal chairs set up for the program, I wandered among stony relics. As I climbed up the steps of the Temple of Warriors, my eyes rested on this sculpture lit up by the moonbeams. It seemed unmoved by the bloody events it must have witnessed long ago. ❖ It struck me as a fascinating scene of contradictions. I created a mental image that I reinforced with a few flash photographs. Then I sketched the scene, marking the highlights accentuated by the silvery light of the full moon. Scratchboard appealed to me as the best medium to capture the essence of what I had experienced.

conquistadors arrived, the Maya city of Chichen Itza was a deserted ruin. This lost world of the Maya remained a secret of the Mesoamerican jungles until European explorers rediscovered it in the mid-nineteenth century.

MIGHTY MONUMENTS

The pyramid called El Castillo — or the Castle, as the Spanish knew it — is probably the most striking feature of the "newer" complex (page 192). Towering at nearly eighty feet, the pyramid has four sides and a platform on the top. Each of the four sides has 91 steps, and the platform itself brings the total number of steps to 365; each step thus marks a day of the year.

Was this an ancient observatory of some sorts? No one really knows. Every year, during the March and September equinoxes, sunbeams strike the northern wall, streaking down to a stone head of Kukulcan (page 195), the feathered snake-god at the base, creating an illusion of a serpent slithering down the stairway towards the sacred cenote. Thousands of people gather every year to watch this spectacular phenomenon.

I huffed and puffed my way up those steep steps to the top of El Castillo. A small entrance led me to another claustrophobic climb to an inner pyramid. Atop a stone platform stood a jaguar throne painted red with inlays of jade and conch. This may have been an altar of yore. A chac mool, a recumbent warrior figure holding a plate, awaited his offering of blood and a beating heart on behalf of the gods (left). Some believe that the offerings of the Maya at one time were corn and flowers, but the Toltec influence introduced gorier offerings of human sacrifice.

Our group was soon in the vast courtyard. It turned out to be an acoustic wonder.

"Listen to this." Facing the pyramid, Ariel clapped his hands. I was stunned as the clap echoed back, sounding like seven shrieks from the rare quetzal bird.

Ariel faced the Temple of Warriors. "Now this!" he exclaimed, clapping

Should I Trust You?: Brown Pelican, Tulum

Scratchboard, 10 x 8

I was in the seaside town of Tulum, two-and-a-half hours by bus from Chichen Itza. I had never come across a gigantic creature staring at me from such uncomfortably close quarters. ✦ Probably more than five feet long, its wings flapped at a span wider than eight feet as it swooped upon a boulder at pecking distance. The graceful bird sized me up, it's blue, beady eyes intently locked into mine. I froze, staying away from the reach of any art or photography paraphernalia lest I be maimed by beak for my transgression. ✦ After several long unrelenting moments, it let down its guard, allowing me to capture a few images digitally. The thrill of the moment was unforgettable. ✦ A well-informed bird specialist later educated me that the Brown pelican is really the smaller of the eight pelican species that inhabit our planet. ✦ I enjoyed scratching its plumage with a #11 X-Acto blade, but found its elastic throat pouch the most complicated area to scratch out!

his hands again. It did seem as though a quetzal shrieked from within the shrine. However, the sound seemed to quickly dart towards the pyramid, and I could hear the same avian shrieks issuing from the monument.

Past the Temple of Venus, we came across a strikingly scary parapet with skull figurines carved all over it. Under the Temple of the Skulls, or the Tzompantli as the Maya called it, were found remains of priests buried over the years. Legend runs that after a conquest of their enemies, the victorious Maya would offer their prisoners for sacrifice and spike their heads upon this platform for display.

The Temple of the Warriors is a noteworthy structure with hundreds of carved pillars. In ancient days this might have been a bustling marketplace with a shrine atop. Depictions of warriors from a different ethnicity adorn the columns; were the Maya really aware of the diversity of the human race?

GAME OF THE GODS

A short distance away is one of the most impressive stadiums of the region. The Great Ball Court measures 272 by 199 feet, about the dimensions of a U.S. football field. The Maya played a deadly game of pok-ta-pok whose object was to drive a nine-pound rubber ball through a stony hoop hoisted high upon each sidewall of the court (page 196). The players could use only their hips, head, feet, knees, and elbows — but not their hands. There were seven players on each team, and the game would go on for days and weeks, rain or shine.

One theory says that the victorious captain was sacrificed to the gods by his counterpart from the losing team; this was considered a proud way to enter paradise. I studied a carving depicting an opponent watching seven bloody serpents stream from the severed neck of the winner; the unlucky fellow's head would soon probably be placed upon a spike at the Tzompantli.

RAMBLING IN THE RUINS

I walked among several quaint structures. Ahead of me towered the pyramid of the High Priest where persistent archaeologists discovered an underground passage that ran all the way to the pyramid complex of Yaxuna, about twenty miles away. Passing other monuments, I arrived at the "old" Chichen location. To me, it seemed that a larger, bolder architectural style had given way to something more intricate. These monuments were also on a smaller scale.

El Caracol, the old observatory, was a fascinating place (pages 202-3). It gets its name from the word "snail," and it was easy to see why as I gazed at the intricate spiral steps. These were housed within a massive stone turret

The Snail Incident: El Caracol

Pen on paper, 11 x 14

My family had an interesting experience looking for a vegetarian restaurant in Cancun. Once we started this quest, we very quickly realized that as international as Cancun was, this type of fare was quite uncommon. Search engines and the internet weren't too useful then, so hotel maps and word of mouth led us to where the locals lived and ate — far from the glitz of five-star hotels. ❖ We didn't actually find the restaurant we had set out to locate, but we spotted a handwritten placard in the window of a different restaurant proclaiming that freshly cooked vegetarian food was available. It was run by a family devoted to the Indian spiritual master Sai Baba. With such an ethnic connection, we struck a bond made easy by the generous hospitality found in these parts of the world. At the end of the meal, the host offered us a gift of a caracol — a snail embossed on a round piece of stone about an inch in diameter. ❖ I didn't recognize the significance of this gift until we visited El Caracol the next day in the Chichen Itza complex. An ancient observatory within a ruin, the Spanish gave this name to the spiral staircase that twists inside. Precise astronomers, the Maya had calculated the revolution of Venus and many other events to a startlingly accurate mathematical degree. Over twenty such celestial events have been recorded on these walls. I could easily imagine these early people peering through the slits, their accurate apparatus in hand. ❖ I used a pointillist approach to capture this esoteric edifice, employing simple black dots using a Sharpie pen on pad. Anish, twelve years old at the time, stepped into the frame to look for a good place to climb!

War and Peace: Girl with a Flower

Acrylic on paper, 12 x 16

The climb to the top of the pyramid was not easy. Amrita, then six years old, clambered up easily along the sharp — and to me rather scary — gradient, while I huffed and puffed along behind her. The sheer incline made it quite a heart-stopping experience to later descend down to the ground, but a rope grip strung from the top let us slower ones step down carefully, holding the line as a support. ❖ Long ago, the high priest — for only the most senior among them was allowed to ascend these structures — would have climbed the stairway to the top amid the sounds of prayers and drumbeats. Victims of sacrifice would have awaited their horrific end. Images of valor and death peered down from the columns. The ominous drumbeats would have reached a crescendo . . . ❖ But now, the scene was soothingly different. Amrita had picked up a flower from somewhere and stood holding it as she gazed serenely from her perch. The Temple of Warriors stood like a mystical castle from time immemorial. Camera-toting tourists were milling around where warlike denizens once demanded blood so that their lands might be blessed with abundance from the gods above. Clouds loomed overhead — soon to bring the rain the Maya had so longed for. The snake-god carving on the pillar seemed to be taking this all in too! ❖ My daughter and I were uninterrupted in that quiet spot for almost fifteen minutes before a tour bus arrived below, disgorging literally dozens of energetic youngsters who promptly made the climb to where we stood. ❖ I later painted this with acrylic, using a fan brush to create those blotches in the sky and the stretch of the Yucatan landscape.

that led up to a platform with several viewing slits facing the skies.

"The snail was one of the four legendary Maya deities, or bacabs, that stood at each corner of the world and supported the firmament," Ariel explained. "It is from here that the ancient Maya would have observed the moon and the stars, and tracked the course of the morning star with amazing accuracy."

A short walk led us to the Cenote Sagrado, the sacred sinkhole of the Maya. Covered by moss and algae, it was probably sixty feet deep and had been used for religious and ceremonial purposes. The Maya considered the cenote's waters to be the abode of the rain god to which they dedicated sacrifices and offerings. It was here that the Maya routinely drowned a sacrificial victim, offering votive oblations of precious stones along with human remains.

"The lives of the Maya — just like these huge structures — are shrouded in mystery." Ariel had to raise his voice above the fluting winds. A peaceful agricultural community, these people had a precise calendar and a hieroglyphic language. They plotted the movements of the planets, and they mastered pottery and weaving. While the culture flourished between 600 and 800 C.E., external influences seem to have transformed tranquility into wars and the practice of human sacrifice. Starting around the beginning of the tenth century, the Maya civilization saw a period of decadence and social upheaval. When the Spanish arrived in Mexico in 1517, they snuffed out a non-Christian culture and, worse still, destroyed thousands of manuscripts replete with the lore and knowledge of those times.

THE EVENING SETTING

It was late afternoon as the sunbeams sloped down the walls of El Castillo, which was dotted with people climbing up its steps. It seemed strange to me that I was looking at the same lintels that the priests from a thousand years ago would have revered. It seemed odd that I walked the stony paths along which sacrificial victims would have trudged, on their way to Eternal Happiness! ❖

A Historical Escape:
Temple of the Winds, Tulum

Watercolor pencil and brush on paper, 11 x 14

Past more watchtowers and iguanas, I ended up at The Temple of the Winds in Tulum. North of Tulum's own El Castillo, this shrine was perched over huge limestone bluffs above the cove that the Maya may have used as a landing spot. There may have been a bustling market in those days when canoes laden with jaguar skins, tobacco, and cacao beans would have departed with shells, fish, and honey fresh from Tulum. ❖ Ariel mentioned this temple may also have served as a warning system for hurricanes in those days. In 1995, he said, when Hurricane Roxanne went by Tulum, the structure made a whistling noise. ❖ The largest Maya archeological site built on the coast, Tulum is not without its detractors. Built in the post-classic period of Maya culture, it lacks the majesty of Tikal or Palenque or the architectural intricacies of Uxmal or Chichen Itza. But for me, the sight of those ancient sentinels atop the limestone crags was one of breathtaking beauty. ❖ Turquoise waters sprayed spume athwart those craggy rocks even as a flock of startled pelicans winged their way across the sky. White sands yawned everywhere along the endless coast. A tourist had somehow slipped away from the guides and audio tours and lectures on history, and made his way past the barricade to simply sit upon a rocky bluff and enjoy the spirit of the moment. ❖ Inspired by the stillness and peace, I painted this on the spot using a set of watercolor pencils and applying seawater (yes!) and brush on my pad. The spongy effect of the rocks was best captured using the wet-on-wet technique.

Paradise on Earth: An Afternoon in Tulum

Watercolor pencil and brush on paper, 11 x 14 (above)

Ink and wash on paper, 11 x 14 (right)

Was this the legendary Maya paradise on earth? ❖ I clambered up to this rocky outcrop, viewing Tulum's El Castillo from the Temple of the Winds. These shrines and watchtowers would have witnessed scenes both routine and bizarre over the years. This structure towers atop a forty-foot bluff above the beach, facing the fleck of palaces and smaller monuments. ❖ As a cool breeze muffled the splash of the waters, I could well imagine the uncontained excitement of the first Spaniard, Juan de Grijalva, who sailed to Tulum. The Castillo and its ramparts, then painted bright red with blue and white motifs, must have gleamed in the setting sun. Apart from being a sacred structure, ⇨

it may have also served as a beacon; lit with huge torches, it would help the Maya in their wooden canoes, journeying from the islands nearby, to keep from straying towards treacherous reefs. These curious traders would have sailed towards the Spanish Armada laden with their treasured cacao beans and pearls, driven only by innocuous hospitality. The rest is sad history . . . ❖ The place resembled a picture postcard: palm trees, sun and sand, all the elements that make for a true vacation paradise. A palm tree had made itself bold, eagerly bending forward, cutting the vista in half. Agave sprang up everywhere as did other lush green shrubbery, lending verdant vigor to the landscape. ❖ I wanted to use light colors, to paint the picture as the fantasy it seemed to be. Almost without conscious thought, I decided to use watercolor pencils with a light wash, leaving most of the pencil strokes intact. ❖ I did another drawing of the El Castillo facade using an ink and brush on paper.

Monk's Prayer on a Surreal Morning
Wat Mahathat from Wat Tra Phang Ngoen

Watercolor, 18 x 24

This was indeed a dreamlike scene. As sacred chants in the Pali language wafted from across the pond, an early-morning fog enveloped the landscape. In the distance I could make out the tall spires of Wat Mahathat and a few stone guardians that kept vigilant watch and blessed the pious. A lone monk clad in ocher robes was offering his worship at a Buddha shrine. ❖ As my guide chattered away with historical facts and architectural details, I lost him to the rapturous sight before me. In this special moment, there wasn't any need for dogma or man-made faith — just the joy of being there and my gratitude for being able to both relish and capture it. Words couldn't do it justice, nor brushstrokes make fair representation; the canvas here was infinitely more vast, handled by an artist with far more skill and expertise, and blessed with a color palette more intricate than a human hand could ever hope to mix. ❖ Nonetheless, I later sketched this scene and coated my cold-pressed paper with eight layers of washes before I could even faintly recreate what I had witnessed that morning. ❖ I returned to Wat Tra Phang Ngoen a bit later in the day to find the scene looking very different — the sun was now smiling down, bringing light to reveal every historical detail that an enthusiast could revel in! ❖ The artist's mystery that had so enchanted me was now a thing of the past.

CHAPTER TWELVE

THAILAND ❖ SUKHOTHAI

DIVINITY IN STONE

Scattered throughout the quiet grounds were watchful Buddhas as far as I could see.

As I pedaled my rusty loaner bicycle past the ruins of temples, funerary monuments, and ancient palaces — now a site of hushed slumber — I couldn't help wondering how this ancient symbol of Thai power could, according to legend, have sent an invading Burmese army fleeing in terror.

Then I saw the thirty-five-foot tall colossus sitting in contemplative meditation under the famous fig tree.

And I understood.

Distant Buddhist chants wafted with the breeze that rippled across the pond of Wat Mahathat that Saturday morning. It seemed those gigantic figures were watching my every movement across this labyrinth of sacred spots: gigantic Buddhas towered everywhere, some seated in calm meditation, many standing in benediction, a few posed as if walking in meditative reflection, and some stretched in silent repose.

I was taking in the vast sanctity of the historical park in ancient Sukhothai. Derived from *Sukhodaya* — which means *the blessed dawn of happiness* — this once-flourishing city was the first capital of Thailand.

It must have been an auspicious day, for Buddhist monks in ocher robes scurried about the Wat Mahathat complex where every shrine had a story to tell. (Views of the complex are on pages 210 and 214-5)

"*Wat* means *temple* in Thai," remarked Maew, my sprightly guide, "and Wat Mahathats all across Thailand are notable for having a relic of the ancient master hidden somewhere among their stonework."

Given how extensive this fantastical twelfth-century complex is, I was surprised at how few licensed guides were available. Fifty-year-old Maew was one of just a handful working in this vast array of structures that dates from the twelfth century C.E.

The day before, I had flown to Bangkok where the temperature was a balmy ninety degrees Fahrenheit. The winter in Chicago had been especially severe, and I barely escaped O'Hare Airport in the aftermath of yet another raging snowstorm. Once in Bangkok, a late afternoon flight took me far away from the city hubbub to a charming private airport in Sukhothai.

After a night in a hotel that stood upon stilts over ponds laden with enchanting lily fronds as well as sonorously persistent mosquitoes, I pedaled my somewhat dilapidated rented bicycle in the predawn darkness towards the park. I met the smiling Maew by the entrance, eager to get started.

In a breathtaking display of nearly two hundred ruins spread over twenty-seven square miles, the Sukhothai Historical Park is speckled with ancient stupas and chedis — mounds where sacred Buddhist relics are housed. There are many viharas or monasteries, Khmer temples, and statues from long ago. Monks would have walked in meditation along the pillared hallways or studied the sacred scriptures while seated on one of the stone benches that lined temple courtyards.

Looking at my map, I realized I was in the central section of the park, teeming with the ruins of twenty-six different shrines and palaces that have stood here

A Forgotten Beauty: Khmer Shrine

Scratchboard, 12 x 16

There is a concentration of man-made wonders in the Sukhothai Historical Park that is replete with shrines and pavilions, ordination halls where individuals were welcomed to the holy order, and burial monuments. However, there were earlier kingdoms that thrived in these parts — some extending north to majestic Pagan in Burma and inimitable Angkor in Cambodia. In these ancient lands, there were no artificial boundaries or border fences. Great monuments and places of worship sprang up wherever colonies expanded and kings conquered. ❖ Some structures would be remembered for an inscription that unveiled something unknown. Others would be revered for a relic buried deep inside and a few for their architectural scale that exquisitely set them apart from lone monuments forgotten in the sweep of time. ❖ Somewhere along the way, I came across this deserted Khmer beauty. Grass and vines now smother the stones, making the scene very different from an auspicious moment in its history when throngs must have gathered in prayer as a nobleman made his offerings to the gods in celebration of a successful conquest. ❖ A curious sparrow flitted among the columns. I took a few photographs for the details, but I later used scratchboard and a scalpel to reveal the temple's fine carvings. This effort took me several days, and I made sure I didn't forget my avian friend who kept me company on that morning's endeavor.

Land of a Thousand Shrines
Wat Mahathat

Acrylic, 16 x 20

I came upon this sight from across a mossy pond full of water lilies. Behind me was the rubble of Noen Prasat, which once had been a large palace where kings and princes walked in pomp, and queens and princesses emerged from palanquins with their retinue of handmaidens. ❖ *These are the largest ruins in the complex and also the most venerated due to the relic of the Buddha buried somewhere among these stones. The procession of stupas and chedis — mounds where sacred Buddhist relics are housed — as well as pavilions and ordination halls with gigantic statues of Buddha make Wat Mahathat a majestic sight.* ❖ *As my guide, Maew, explained: this is where the Buddha icons take on special sculptural attributes. The Buddhas shown standing or walking are very typical of Sukhothai, as is his typical smile of serenity. "The Ayutthaya Buddha has a more severe expression," Maew said. The lotus-bud shape on the finials is a Sukhothai original, and so is the signature flame on Buddha's head.* ❖ *Here was a scene set in the Buddha's era.* ❖ *I took a few photographs and later painted this vista in acrylic.*

Canine Karma:
Lone Sentinel, Wat Sra Si

Scratchboard, 12 x 16

This was my second attempt at sketching this scene. My first, ten years prior, was an embarrassing fiasco thanks to the canine colony of Sukhothai. ❖ A video camera in hand, I was happily filming the golden sunrise by the shrine. When I heard the clip-clop of galloping paws behind me, I froze in fear. A pack of strays materialized from nowhere and began circling me, the bolder ones gnashing their teeth and nipping at my heels. ❖ My savior came in the form of a Thai jogger. The strays quickly turned their attention upon the poor soul and gave chase. I watched with concern as the clever fellow twisted around and screamed something in Thai. The dogs whimpered and promptly trotted away. ❖ For this second trip, I admit I was glad to have my guide along with me. It felt nice to have a bodyguard as a few strays still haunted the area. ❖ I took a few photos and completed my sketch in charcoal. Back in Chicago, I attempted a scratchboard in order to depict the texture of stones and the silent guardian who had once witnessed my attack but had chosen not to intervene! ❖ Commenting on the events of my first trip, some of my Thai colleagues speculated that the jogger had magically materialized to finally put an end my bad karma, something I was divinely ordained to endure. ❖ I wonder.

for the last eight centuries. This area, slightly bigger than a single square mile, is cut off from the remainder of the park by three rings of encircling walls that are themselves encircled by a wide moat.

As with many civilizations in Southeast Asia, Thailand's history is just as hazy as the early-morning fog that shrouded the Sukhothai complex that morning.

Many cultures have walked these lands across thousands of years. However, it is well known that the mighty Khmer Empire from Angkor held sway in these parts through the early part of the thirteenth century.

Two resolute brothers, Pra Khun Bangklanghao and Pra Khun Phameung, finally overthrew the Khmer chieftain, establishing the first truly independent kingdom in Thai history in 1238 C.E., which then flourished for just over two hundred years.

Through conquests and alliances, the kingdom soon expanded its boundaries and achieved tremendous prosperity, reaching a glorious age in arts, crafts, and literary lore during the reign of the much-venerated King Ramkhamhaeng around the latter part of the thirteenth century. This erudite monarch even created the first Thai script. Maew took me to the spot where a replica of the stela stands today. However, clearly the alphabet or the language has changed since then, for my guide struggled to decipher what was inscribed!

During the time of this king, a powerful triangle formed among the kingdom of Pagan in Burma, the Khmer civilization of Angkor in Cambodia, and glorious Sukhothai, stretching from Laos to the northern part of present-day Thailand and south to the Malay Peninsula. Thai merchants excelled in trade, especially with China and the Far East; they also took their wares to the Persian Empire and even across to the frontiers of Europe. Monks from Sri Lanka, China, and other Buddhist strongholds frequently interacted with the Thai people. Architectural traditions were exchanged as well as the tenets of Theravada Buddhism, which came to be the predominant religious philosophy of the people in the kingdom—a characteristic of Thailand that is still true today.

The Mango Incident: Colossus of Wat Si Chum

Whiteboard and ink, 14 x 19

This is probably one of the most intriguing shrines in the complex. From a distance it seems like yet another plain structure outside the western Or Gate. As I approached the monument, however, a gigantic face appeared between a slit in the enclosure. ❖ I simply stood in stupefied wonder at the thirty-five-foot colossus, even as the Burmese soldiers of the legends may have frozen, coming literally face to face with the unexpected before fleeing in terror. As I walked into the narrow sanctum, dappled sunlight lit up a beaming smile on the master's countenance. This powerful Buddha of Wat Sri Chum was known as Phra Achana — the fearless one. ❖ I later stepped out into the vast courtyard where once there may have been a large meditation hall with monks in prayer. I noticed a huge mango tree generously shedding its unripe green fruit and couldn't resist the urge to crunch a few between my teeth. Enjoyable as it seemed then, the sap left an ulcerous reminder on my tongue for a couple of weeks, long after the taste was totally gone. ❖ I backed up to take in the view from outside the shrine and made a quick sketch, noting the play of light upon the face — especially how the mother-of-pearl eyeballs lent a certain calmness to the exquisitely perfect features. ❖ I made a quick drawing with a sepia Conté crayon, but decided that the effect of carved stone was best rendered with the scratch technique. I used scalpel on whiteboard, coloring this in with several coats of ink.

BUDDHAS GALORE

By the end of the day, I had visited more than fifty temples across five sections of the complex, even climbing up to a hill shrine on the periphery of town. I had started from my hotel located to the east of the complex, went past Wat Mahathat and the three-spired Khmer structure of Wat Si Sawai, then walked towards Wat Sra Si (page 216), which is situated upon an island. The elephant spire of Wat Sorasak (pages 224-5) looks quietly over the vast sprawl of ancient stones.

In the northern section, past the old city walls, is the shrine of Wat Si Chum and its gigantic Buddha (left), which, according to a popular tale, once brought a threatening Burmese contingentt to a sudden stop. Many shrines are sprinkled in the western section past Or Gate, notably the Khmer ruins of Wat Tuk, ancient Wat Mongkorn, and the sacred colossus upon the hill where lay the ruins of Wat Saphan Hin (pages 220-1).

Pedaling my bicycle in the southern section, I was most impressed by the slate temple of Wat Chetupon, where enormous Buddhas watched me from every nook, and, adjacent to it, the handsome shrine of Wat Chedi Si Hong (page 222). Many sacred spots dot the east, from where I'd come, but the shrine of Wat Chang Lom — with its magnificent elephants and a lone shrub growing atop the spire — made it a picturesque setting.

"Sukhothai's pottery was truly inimitable," Maew remarked while we were visiting the Sangkhalok Museum later that afternoon. As we looked at the exhibits, it became clear that there was a time when hundreds of artisans busied themselves with their kilns, firing pots, and plates — wares bound for distant lands.

Soon after the death of King Ramkhamhaeng, vassals and tributary states broke away. The influence of the powerful Ayutthaya Kingdom in the south began eroding the foundations of an empire that had already lost its luster.

Surprise at the Top:
Wat Saphan Hin

Conté crayon, 14 x 17

"Seated upon an elephant, King Ramkhamhaeng used to climb up to this shrine to offer his worship on Buddhist holy days," Maew commented. He seemed remarkably unconcerned that I was struggling to keep my foothold on the narrow slate steps leading to the top of the seven-hundred-foot hill that jutted up from the plains. He himself was as nimble as a goat. ❖ The thought of hefty elephants tromping up these loose stone slabs was a bewildering one. Maybe these slabs had become weathered with time? ❖ Aptly meaning "stone bridge," the compact complex of Wat Saphan Hin is located outside the western city wall, far away from the hubbub of tourists that sunny morning. A lone British tourist was making his ascent. ❖ As we reached the crest of the hill, I realized that a colossus had been serenely watching my climb: a standing Buddha, nearly forty feet tall. A smaller Buddha sat calmly by his feet, surrounded by several stark columns, remnants from a magnificent structure of yore. It was an intriguing glimpse into how powerfully this shrine might have affected the devout in those times. ❖ I walked around the complex and noticed that a tall concrete beam, probably recently erected, was holding the standing Buddha aloft from the back. Nearby was a beautiful yellow cotton tree whose flowers had scattered in the winds, speckling the ground with a brilliant dust of petals. ❖ I descended the steps to cast a parting look at the watchful guardian. It was blazing bright and searing hot by then, and nothing more than a photograph could have worked for me.

Reliving a Past

It was late evening when I clanked my bicycle back towards the large complex of Wat Mahathat. I wanted to witness the spectacle of the sun sinking below the spires. A huge Buddha sat in silence across a glistening pond, just as it had for over eight hundred years. In my mind's eye, I pictured several other figures that may have graced this landscape but over time were shipped in long barges towards Bangkok to be installed in that region's newer temples.

There was a lot of activity that evening at Wat Sra Si (page 208). I was fortunate

The Four-Roomed Shrine: Wat Chedi Si Hong

Whiteboard painted with acrylic and ink, 12 x 16

As I mouthed out loud the words on the posted sign, Maew asked me how I could pronounce Thai so well. ❖ As we had walked in the scorching heat from Wat Chetupon towards this next monument complex, I told him an anecdote from my very first day of a five year work stint in beautiful Bangkok in the nineties. ❖ "Phom . . . Dichaan . . .," I had stuttered over the phone, English–Thai phrasebook in hand, to what must have been a consternated pizza-store employee on the listening end. Little did I realize that the manual indicated that "phom" was a male "I," and "dichaan" a female "I," and I could not possibly belong to both genders at the same time! The order did arrive, however, but was quite different from what I had attempted to request. Nor for that matter had my attempts at Thai meant much to the delivery man — so much so that I handed him a big note, and all I got in return was a signature Thailand smile, but no change. And I didn't know how to ask for it! ❖ By the time my story ended, we had arrived at the beautiful shrine of Wat Chedi Si Hong. I proudly announced that "si hong" meant "four rooms" in Thai and could sense that Maew's respect for me multiplied that very instant! ❖ I found several things very intriguing about the structure, and they inspired me to open my sketchbook. The main chedi looked beautiful without its spire, and I thought the vertical stone "blinds" in an adjacent enclosure were a very creative idea. Long ago, each slat could have been individually adjusted to let in the breeze from across the sunny landscape outdoors. ❖ Wanting to capture the bright colors that afternoon, I decided that black and white scratchboard wasn't the right medium. I tried out a technique that I had never done before on this scale: painting a whiteboard with acrylic colors and using a scalpel to scratch out the details. So that the white underneath wouldn't show, I had to repeatedly apply light washes with ink.

enough to be visiting during one of the only eight nights each year when a sound and light show is held with the Wat as the backdrop. As I hurried to find the driest spot on the island across the way, musicians began the slow lilt of a bygone time. As the skies darkened, the Wat lit up as the program began with a reenactment of life from long ago.

Graceful apsaras danced just as they would have in the times of Khmer glory. Armies marched in, warriors descending upon the city with their weaponry, and these lands soon came to be conquered. With all that pomp of music and show of fireworks, the great Sukhothai Kingdom had begun to flourish. At that moment I witnessed a surreal sight I will never forget: dozens of tall, colorful paper lanterns, propelled only

"Wat Sorasak"

Elephant Procession, Wat Sorasak

Conté crayon, 14 x 17

I was walking in the central part of the Sukhothai Historical Park when I chanced upon this masterpiece in the deserted shrine of Wat Sorasak. Commissioned to be built in the early 1400s by a monk named Nai Inthara Sorasak, its purpose was to honor the governor. ❖ This could have been a scene from ancient Sri Lanka. The influence of that country's architectural motifs was unmistakable, from the stroke of the chisel to the slather of the trowel. ❖ In awe, I gazed at the parade of twenty-four stucco elephants that protectively emerged from the bricks holding up the chedi. "These elephants," Maew told me, "are eternally upholding our great tenets of Buddhism." ❖ The bricks that make up the base have been worn away by six hundred years of exposure to the elements, but the stucco was firmly holding up the line of resolute pachyderms. ❖ I would have liked to do a quick sketch, but the mosquito orchestra was getting a bit sonorous and aggressive. A photograph seemed like the most painless option at hand. ❖ Later, I made this drawing in a couple of hours in the air-conditioned comfort of my room.

by flames and smoke, rose up high into the skies to the magical accompaniment of light and sound.

It was if I had been transported to a celebration of ancient times. As these radiant objects bobbed their ways up and soared high, it seemed as though the sky was lit by a group of man-made stars clumped together to form a beautiful constellation. The royal family and their entourage watched the spectacle from a balcony.

The program continued, quickly taking us to a time in the mid–fifteenth century when the mighty kingdom of Ayutthaya, located to the south, enveloped this culture in a bloodless war, creating a new era in Thai history. Soon after, the festivities ended, the lights dimmed, and all was quiet again.

Here in Sukhothai, these hundreds of Buddhas set upon lofty perches watched change upon change, century by century. Kings had come and gone, armies were vanquished and treasures looted. These ever-present eyes watched it all. ✦

Finally, An Elephant Sighting!: Si Satchanalai

Scratchboard, 16 x 12

Living in Thailand for nearly five years, I adopted the common mode of transport and took the motorcycle taxi or simply the "motorcy" as it is known in local parlance. Like everyone else, I'd weave furiously through the dense Bangkok traffic, clinging to the handlebars for dear life. Several times on Bangkok's main street — Sukhumvit Road — I had come close enough to tickle an elephant on its leg. But at some point, they stopped these animals from plodding the streets of Bangkok. Now I was back for a brief visit, having lived over fifteen years in Chicago, and I longed to come across an elephant again. ✦ I desperately called up a well-known elephant sanctuary in Sukhothai. However, they would accommodate only guests who stayed over in their accommodations so these gentle giants could bond with the visitors. Even if I was able and willing to do that, their location was more than an hour away from the ruins, and it wouldn't serve my purpose given that my time there was short. ✦ My guide, Maew, was eager to help me in my quest. We could, he said, wander the forests of Si Satchanalai in search of elephants that often emerged out of the thickets in search of sugarcane fields. He even suggested the far-fetched notion of lying in wait in one such clearing, from which, he assured me, a trumpeting herd would emerge during the sunset hours. Alas, those forests were more than six hours away, and in such sweltering heat, it wasn't the most appealing of options. ✦ Out of the blue, we bumped into a mahout by the name of Tong, who was ambling towards a welcome patch of shade with his handsome charge. Tong was headed home to his village, located between Sukhothai and Si Satchanalai. ✦ Happy at my good fortune, I took a few pictures of Tong and his pachyderm companion — simply known as Nok. As a token of my gratitude, I gave Nok a bunch of bananas I had tucked away in the van. ✦ A month later, I recreated this scene on scratchboard, using a line tool to capture the soft yet wrinkly skin.

K.V. Krishnan

AFTERWORD

Change is an inevitable consequence of time, though it can be hard to accept that the old does eventually gives way to the new.

Even the best researched travelogue cannot foretell how places might be transformed: an ancient monument in the Holy Land may get a facelift to appease the crowds of tourists; a wobbly Buddhist monolith in ancient Sukhothai could be propped up with an ugly concrete beam held in place by a labyrinth of steel railings; an ancient Maya artifact may be newly discovered in Actun Tunichil Muknal, entirely changing our views on a particular period in history; or a scenic viewpoint in Hawaii could be shut down due to an angry volcanic outburst.

Over the years I've spent a lot of time and energy researching the places I visit, engaging the best guides and historians available. None of this changes the fact that there could be another startling discovery tomorrow that could change the way we view things today. Altered by time, flavored by piety or fervor, legends are often notoriously mixed with history, giving long-ago people and their deeds a larger-than-life outlook. As much as possible I have tried my best to separate the two and yet keep my work informative and compelling.

I am hoping my readers will excuse me for any visual or literary omissions and transgressions and will simply enjoy this book as an adventurous excursion into the divine.

Images

BELIZE ✤ ACTUN TUNICHIL MUKNAL

(18) *Should I or Should I Not?: At the Entrance to the Cave.* 9 x 12 inches (22.9 x 30.5 cm). Scratchboard.

(20) *Mother and Child: A Family Portrait.* 16 x 20 inches (40.6 x 50.8 cm). Scratchboard.

(22) *Speleological Spectacle: A Massive Flowstone.* 12 x 9 inches (30.5 x 22.9 cm). Charcoal.

(23) *A Rare Guest?: Feisty Harpy Eagle.* 14 x 10 inches (35.6 x 25.4 cm). Watercolor.

(24) *Evil Banished.* 9 x 14 inches (22.9 x 35.6 cm). Pastel.

(25) *A Horrific Death: Victim of a Sacrifice.* 5 x 7 inches (12.7 x 17.8 cm). Scratchboard.

(27) *Shimmering Splendor: Giants of the Cathedral.* 9 x 12 inches (22.9 x 30.5 cm). Scratchboard and ink.

(28) *Oh, What a Horrific End!: Sacrificial Remains by the Flowstone Monoliths.* 11 x 14 inches (27.9 x 35.6 cm). Watercolor.

(29) *Beauty in the Wild: Brazilian Red Cloak.* 14 x 11 inches (35.6 x 27.9). *Colored pencil.*

(30) *End of an Adventure: Welcome Back to the Human World!* 11 x 14 inches (27.9 x 35.6 cm). Watercolor.

CAMBODIA ✤ ANGKOR

(32) *Clink of Anklets: Apsara Lintel, Hall of the Dancers, Preah Khan.* 18 x 14 inches (45.7 x 35.6 cm). Graphite on paper.

(35) *5:30 A.M.: Sunrise at Angkor Wat.* 10 x 14 inches (25.4 x 35.6 cm). Watercolor.

(36) *Serpent Shock: Library, Preah Khan.* 9 x 12 inches (22.9 x 30.5 cm). Scratchboard and ink.

(37) *The Divine Stranglehold.* 11 x 8 inches (27.9 x 20.3 cm). Pastel on paper.

(38) *Watchful Eyes: Avalokiteswara Heads of Bayon.* 9 x 12 inches (22.9 x 30.5 cm). Scratchboard.

(41) *Souvenir Girl: Glorious Brick Shrines of Pre-Rup.* 14 x 18 inches (35.6 x 45.7 cm). Pen and ink on paper.

(43) *Do Not Disturb: Deity, Ta Prohm.* 10 x 14 inches (25.4 x 35.6 cm). Ink on paper.

(44) *Too Close for Comfort: Spung Tree at Ta Prohm.* 16 x 20 inches (40.6 x 50.8 cm). Acrylic on paper.

UNITED STATES OF AMERICA ✤ HAWAII

(46) *Tryst of the Sisters: Pele Meets Nāmaka.* 12 x 16 inches (30.5 x 40.6 cm). Acrylic on paper.

(49) *10:00 p.m.: View from Jaggar Museum Overlook.* 10 x 12 inches (25.4 x 30.5 cm). Pastel on board.

(50) *Fury of the Pu'u 'O'o Vent.* 8 x 10 inches (20.3 x 25.4 cm). Scratchboard and ink.

(52)   *The Firepit of Halema'uma'u.* 12 x 16 inches (30.5 x 40.6 cm). Acrylic on paper.

(54)   *Lava Ladies: Nene Mother and Gosling.* 12 x 16 inches (30.5 x 40.6 cm). Scratchboard.

(57)   *Lazy Ladybugs: Lehua Blossom.* 10 x 8 inches (25.4 x 20.3 cm). Pastel.

INDIA ❖ VARANASI

(58)   *Fire and Smoke, the End of It All: Manikarnika Ghat.* 16 x 20 inches (40.6 x 50.8 cm). Acrylic on hardboard.

(60)   *The Umbrella Parade.* 12 x 16 inches (30.5 x 40.6 cm). Scratchboard.

(62)   *A Surprise Guest.* 11 x 14 inches (27.9 x 35.6 cm). Watercolor.

(64)   *Peacock by a Tea Stall.* 8 x 6 inches (20.3 x 14.4 cm). Scratchboard.

(66)   *Pehlwan and the Sadhu.* 16 x 20 inches (40.6 x 50.8 cm). Acrylic on hardboard.

(69)   *Integration Inconceivable: Gyanvapi Mosque.* 12 x 16 inches (30.5 x 40.6 cm). Scratchboard. 12 x 16 inches (30.5 x 40.6 cm). Sepia wash. 16 x 20 inches (40.6 x 50.8 cm). Pen and ink.

(70)   *The Temple Heist.* 8 x 10 inches (20.3 x 25.4 cm). Scratchboard.

(73)   *Paintings in the Making: Wanderings of a Young Artist.* 20 x 16, 16 x 20 inches (40.6 x 50.8 cm). Pen on paper.

(74)   *A Riot of Color: Kedar Ghat.* 16 x 20 inches (40.6 x 50.8 cm). Acrylic on hardboard.

GUATEMALA ❖ TIKAL

(76)   *Jewels in the Forest: View from Temple IV.* 9 x 12 inches (22.9 x 30.5 cm). Whiteboard and ink.

(78)   *The Morning Greeting.* 14 x 11 inches (35.6 x 27.9 cm). Watercolor.

(79)   *Toucan Snacking by Mundo Perdido.* 12 x 9 inches (30.5 x 22.9 cm). Whiteboard and ink.

(81)   *A Tall Majesty: View of Temple IV.* 11 x 14 inches (27.9 x 35.6 cm). Conté crayon.

(82)   *The Moonlight Supper.* 10 x 12 inches (25.4 x 30.5 cm). Pastel on board.

(85)   *Pedro, King of the Swamp.* 12 x 9 inches (30.5 x 22.9 cm). Colored pencil.

(86)   *Drama upon Stone: Sunset behind Temple II, Viewed from the North Acropolis.* 11 x 14 inches (27.9 x 35.6 cm). Acrylic on canvas board.

(89)   *Peeping through the Rock: A Temple IV Vista.* 11 x 14 inches (27.9 x 35.6 cm). Watercolor.

(92)   *A Curious Visitor: Sunset on the Temple of the Great Jaguar.* 11 x 14 inches (27.9 x 35.6 cm). Acrylic on canvas board.

United Kngdom ❖ Stonehenge

(94) *The Hungry Blackbird.* 11 x 14 inches (27.9 x 35.6 cm). Pencil on paper.

(96) *A Girl in Tears: Raven upon a Sarsen.* 9 x 12 inches (22.9 x 30.5 cm). Scratchboard.

(98) *Raucous Shrieks: The Vast Vista.* 16 x 20 inches (40.6 x 50.8 cm). Acrylic on paper.

(100) *Lost My Partner: Lone Heel Stone.* 9 x 12 inches (22.9 x 30.5 cm). Watercolor.

(103) *Closer to the Stones.* 12 x 16 inches (30.5 x 40.6 cm). Watercolor.

(104) *6 P.M.: Sunset through the Stones.* 11 x 14 inches (27.9 x 35.6 cm). Watercolor.

Jordan ❖ Petra

(106) *Eating My Coffee: Evening at Wadi Rum.* 11 x 14 inches (27.9 x 35.6 cm). Pastel on paper.

(109) *Genies Galore: Djinn Blocks.* 12 x 16 inches (30.5 x 40.6 cm). Conté crayon.

(110) *Fruitless Factoids: The Obelisk Tomb and the Bab as-Siq Triclinium.* 11 x 14 inches (27.9 x 35.6 cm). Conté crayon.

(112) *Cliffs on Fire!: Walking into the Gorge.* 14 x 11 inches (35.6 x 27.9 cm). Watercolor.

(114) *Snaking through the Gorge.* 16 x 12 inches (40.6 x 30.5 cm). Scratchboard.

(117) *When the Rocks Yawned Open!* 14 x 11 inches (35.6 x 27.9 cm). Scratchboard and ink.

(118) *Help!: Al-Khazneh from a Ridge.* 14 x 11 inches (35.6 x 27.9 cm). Pen and ink.

(119) *Tributes to the Dead: The Royal Tombs.* 16 x 12 inches (40.6 x 30.5 cm). Scratchboard.

(120) *Two Camels: Along the Colonnaded Street.* 11 x 14 inches (27.9 x 35.6 cm). Conté crayon.

Israel ❖ Holy Land

(122) *Hurried Sketch: The Temple Mount behind the Western Wall, Jerusalem.* 11 x 14 inches (27.9 x 35.6 cm). Acrylic on paper.

(124) *Ramparts Timeless: The Tower of David, Jerusalem.* 12 x 16 inches (30.5 x 40.6 cm). Conté crayon.

(128) *Daunting Gates: Pathways for Ancient Chariots, Megiddo.* 12 x 16 inches (30.5 x 40.6 cm). Conté crayon.

(131) *Done for the Day!: Full Moon Night, Jaffa.* 11 x 14 inches (27.9 x 35.6 cm). Scratchboard.

(134) *Vulture in the Skies: Caves of Sacred Scrolls, Qumran.* 12 x 16 inches (30.5 x 40.6 cm). Watercolor.

(137) *Boy Exploring an Aqueduct: Caesarea.* 11 x 14 inches (27.9 x 35.6 cm). Watercolor.

(138) *The Afternoon Service: View of an Ancient Harbor, Caesarea.* 18 x 24 inches (45.7 x 61.0 cm). Watercolor.

(140) *Pilgrims in Prayer: Church of the Nativity, Bethlehem.* 16 x 20 inches (40.6 x 50.8 cm). Acrylic on board.

(142) *Hic de Virgine Maria Jesus Christus Natus Est: Bethlehem.* 11 x 14 inches (27.9 x 35.6 cm). Watercolor on hot-pressed paper.

(144) *Peace in the Clatter: Sunset at Nazareth.* 16 x 20 inches (40.6 x 50.8 cm). Acrylic.

(147) *The White Synagogue: Capernaum.* 14 x 11 inches (35.6 x 27.9 cm). Scratchboard.

(149) *Light from the Clouds: The Mount of Beatitudes, Capernaum.* 11 x 14 inches (27.9 x 35.6 cm). Watercolor.

(150) *Spice and Color: View of the Harbor, Akko.* 15 x 20 inches (38.1 x 50.8 cm). Watercolor.

(152) *Knight with a Sword: Akko.* 9 x 12 inches (22.9 x 30.5 cm). Watercolor.

(156) *Bastion of the Resolute, Masada.* 11 x 14 inches (27.9 x 35.6 cm). Conté crayon.

EGYPT ❖ GIZA

(158) *Off the Beaten Path: Goliaths of the Desert.* 11 x 14 inches (27.9 x 35.6 cm). Watercolor.

(160) *Camel Catastrophe: Resting from the Ride.* 9 x 12 inches (22.9 x 30.5 cm). Scratchboard.

(162) *A Colossal Pair: The Great Sphinx and the Great Pyramid.* 16 x 20 inches (40.6 x 50.8 cm). Scratchboard.

(164) *Whatever Does It Say?: The Tomb of Ptahhotep.* 11 x 14 inches (27.9 x 35.6 cm). Pen and sepia wash.

(167) *Memento Moment: Djoser's Step Pyramid, Saqqara.* 11 x 14 inches (27.9 x 35.6 cm). Watercolor.

(168) *There It Is!: Step Pyramid from the Valley Temple of Unas, Saqqara.* 11 x 14 inches (27.9 x 35.6 cm). Acrylic on canvas board.

(171) *Sleepy Sentinel: Memphis.* 11 x 14 inches (27.9 x 35.6 cm). Conté crayon.

(172) *Inside the Serapeum: The Catacomb of the Sacred Bulls.* 11 x 14 inches (27.9 x 35.6 cm). India ink and brush.

(174) *Hunting for a Shark: Sunset at Giza.* 12 x 16 inches (30.5 x 40.6 cm). Watercolor.

GREECE ❖ DELPHI

(176) *The Legend of the Oracle.* 18 x 14 inches (45.8 x 35.6 cm). Scratchboard.

(178) *Shaky Start: Ionic Column.* 11 x 14 inches (27.9 x 35.6 cm). Whiteboard and ink.

(180) *Rain Drenched and Light Washed: Verdant Olive Groves.* 11 x 14 inches (27.9 x 35.6 cm). Watercolor.

(183) *An Interrupted Bargain: Treasury of the Athenians.* 14 x 18 inches (35.6 x 45.8 cm). Acrylic.

(184) *Shadow of a Shrine: Pillars of the Temple of Apollo.* 11 x 14 inches (27.9 x 35.6 cm). Conté crayon.

(186) *Rebus Revenge: The Sphinx of Naxos.* 14 x 11 inches (35.6 x 27.9 cm). Conté crayon on cream pastel paper.

(190) *Mathematical Mystery: Tholos.* 14 x 18 inches (35.6 x 45.8 cm). Watercolor.

MEXICO ❖ CHICHEN ITZA

(192) *Rapt Reptile: El Castillo on a Cloudy Day.* 12 x 16 inches (30.5 x 40.6 cm). Acrylic on paper.

(195) *Talking in Smiles: Kukulcan Balustrade.* 9 x 12 inches (22.9 x 30.5 cm). Conté crayon.

(196) *Death for Eternity: Pok-ta-pok Ball Court.* 9 x 12 inches (22.9 x 30.5 cm). Watercolor washes on paper.

(197) *When is Lunch?: Iguana Basking on the Rocks.* 5 x 7 inches (12.7 x 17.8 cm). Scratchboard.

(198) *Heart and Blood: Chac Mool Awaits.* 11 x 14 inches (27.9 x 35.6 cm). Scratchboard.

(200) *Should I Trust You?: Brown Pelican, Tulum.* 10 x 8 inches (25.4 x 20.3 cm). Scratchboard.

(202) *The Snail Incident: El Caracol.* 11 x 14 inches (27.9 x 35.6 cm). Pen on paper.

(204) *War and Peace: Girl with a Flower.* 12 x 16 inches (30.5 x 40.6 cm). Acrylic on paper.

(206) *A Historical Escape: Temple of the Winds, Tulum.* 11 x 14 inches (27.9 x 35.6 cm). Watercolor pencil and brush on paper.

(208) *Paradise on Earth: An Afternoon in Tulum.* 11 x 14 inches (27.9 x 35.6 cm). Watercolor pencil and brush on paper. Ink and wash on paper.

THAILAND ❖ SUKHOTHAI

(210) *Monk's Prayer on a Surreal Morning: Wat Mahathat: from Wat Tra Phang Ngoen.* 18 x 24 inches (45.8 x 61.0 cm). Watercolor.

(213) *A Forgotten Beauty: Khmer Shrine.* 12 x 16 inches (30.5 x 40.6 cm). Scratchboard.

(214) *Land of a Thousand Shrines: Wat Mahathat.* 16 x 20 inches (40.6 x 50.8 cm). Acrylic.

(216) *Canine Karma: Lone Sentinel, Wat Sra Si.* 12 x 16 inches (30.5 x 40.6 cm). Scratchboard.

(218) *The Mango Incident: Colossus of Wat Si Chum.* 14 x 19 inches (35.6 x 48.3 cm). Whiteboard and ink.

(220) *Surprise at the Top: Wat Saphan Hin.* 14 x 17 inches (35.6 x 43.2 cm). Conté crayon.

(222) *The Four-Roomed Shrine: Wat Chedi Si Hong.* 12 x 16 inches (30.5 x 40.6 cm). Whiteboard painted with acrylic and ink.

(224) *Elephant Procession, Wat Sorasak.* 14 x 17 inches (35.6 x 43.2 cm). Conté crayon.

(227) *Finally, An Elephant Sighting!: Si Satchanalai.* 16 x 12 inches (40.6 x 30.5 cm). Scratchboard.

About the Author
KRISH V. KRISHNAN

Consumed by insatiable wanderlust and a deep-rooted passion for exploring exotic cultures, Krish V. Krishnan has lived in or visited over sixty countries and has published more than five hundred articles on travel and humor in various newspapers all over the world.

Krishnan has won a Best Travel Writer of the Year award and also received accolades for raising from obscurity previously little-known places through his writing.

As a global citizen, Krishnan often found himself in strange situations: once being suspected of kidnapping his own son across the Israel-Jordan border, and on another occasion, being grilled by a suspicious Sri Lankan immigration officer who wondered why someone of Indian ethnicity living in Thailand working for a U.S. company engaged in a project in Israel and South Africa would travel to Colombo on business.

As an artist, Krishnan focuses on landscapes and ancient monuments, capturing their essence by using a variety of techniques including scratchboards, watercolors, and acrylic mediums. Over the last thirty years, he has exhibited his artwork in many group and solo shows in the United States and around the world. He has also won several art awards. As a signature member of a number of prestigious artists' organizations, including the International Society of Scratchboard Artists and Artists for Conservation, Krishnan regularly exhibits his work in juried and non-juried shows organized by local art guilds in American cities.

When not holding a pen, brush, or an airplane ticket, Krishnan heads up a global outfit that has him frequently shifting gears between Thai, Hindi, Thinglish, Hinglish and English.

An alumnus of the Harvard Business School, Krishnan lives in Wilmette, Illinois, with his wife and daughter, while he continues to coax his recently graduated son to embark on a study-abroad experience.

ART · NATURE · SPIRIT

SHANTI ARTS celebrates art, nature, and spirit through exhibitions and publications. If you enjoyed this book and would like to find out about our other books, we invite you to visit us online. There you will find a complete list of our books and serial publications as well as information about exhibitions, artist and writer opportunities, and book submissions. Our books may be purchased on our website, through most online booksellers, and at many fine bookstores.

If you would like to receive mailings about our exhibitions and publications, please visit our website and add your name to our mailing list.

shantiarts.com
info@shantiarts.com

CPSIA information can be obtained
at www.ICGtesting.com
Printed in the USA
BVXC01n2043201114
375544BV00003B/3

* 9 7 8 1 9 4 1 8 3 0 9 2 5 *